My Silence Roars

by Tina Jackson

The Advocado Press

2026

Printed in the United States of America. No part of this book may be used or reproduced in any manner whatsoever without written permission.

Published by the Advocado Press in association with the Center for Accessible Living, 501 East Broadway, Suite 301, Louisville, KY 40202

www.advocadopress.org

FIRST EDITION

My Silence Roars
Written by Tina Jackson

Cover design by Hannah Richards
Editing by Dave Matheis

ISBN 978-0-9721189-7-2

What People are Saying About My Silence Roars

Tina's book is an honest look at the many barriers people with disabilities must contend with. She provides a firsthand account of what it takes to remain independent and live life on your own terms, and the power of personal advocacy

- Johnny Callebs, Executive Director, Commonwealth Council on Developmental Disabilities

Bravo to Tina on her debut book and autobiography! This work beautifully documents a young, intelligent woman coming of age in an able-bodied world—one who refuses to let disability or setbacks define or limit her. I truly felt as though I was right there with her as she lived life to the fullest and discovered herself over the years, all while dressed in bell bottoms with flowers in her hair. Peace!

-Camille Collins-Dean, Assistant Director, Kentucky Department of Protection and Advocacy

Tina's book is amazing!

-Carrissa Johnson, CNP, Satellite Office Manager for the Center for Accessible Living

-

Prologue

We all come into this world a "blank slate", then write on it our hopes and dreams for the life we want to live. I was no different. I dreamed of gaining employment, having lots of friends, and learning ways to fit into a world not made for those with disabilities. I dreamed of being independent and helping others find their way to living more independently. My dreams were seemingly coming true, with jobs in the social work field until age 24.

Suppose you woke up one day to discover you could not speak again. Imagine going through just one of your busy days without uttering a word - then imagine the rest of your life in silence. Imagine being told that you could never take another bite of food for fear of aspiration pneumonia. This is the story of how I learned to adjust to multiple challenges, living without a verbal voice, unable to eat or drink like most people do; how I would adapt to the world, and how the world would adapt to me.

"One day, you will tell your story of how you've overcome what you are going through now, and it will become part of someone else's survival."

Dedication

I want to dedicate my memoir to my Mom, Pauline, who had the wisdom to allow me to believe that I could do anything, encouraged me to take risks, and supported my decisions even if she didn't agree with them, and to my Dad, Willie, who taught me the importance of education to my independence and how to handle money.

CONTENTS

POEMS

Chapter 1

"She has to learn to do things herself."

I entered the world a happy baby. But even as a young girl, I knew life would be different for me. I was determined to do whatever it took to live an active and full life. My parents possessed the wisdom to encourage me and the courage to give me the appropriate push I needed to give the extra effort, which in turn gave me the will to succeed. In addition, I inherited a drive to overcome challenges from a long line of ancestors filled with strong, industrious women and ambitious, hard-working men.

My grandparents were farmers and coal miners in rural Elliott and Boyd Counties in Northeastern Kentucky in the foothills of the Appalachian Mountains. About 1920, they moved to nearby Ashland, a small city on the southern bank of the Ohio River at almost the exact point where Kentucky meets Ohio and West Virginia. The city experienced a growth spurt in the 1920s sparked by the construction of a steel mill that featured a continuous rolling method to produce steel sheets. The company who built it was called Armco. Other factories moved into town and it was the new manufacturing jobs that attracted my grandparents to move to the city. Once in Ashland, both of my grandfathers found employment at the Armco Steel Mill where they would work until retirement.

My grandmothers each raised more than ten children during the depression, augmenting their husbands' earnings by tending gardens and raising livestock. The children wore handmade clothing passed down from child to child. In a time when it was uncommon for women to work outside of the home, my Grandmother Leibee, my mother's mother, was a cook at the elementary school.

My Papaw Blevins, my father's father, never learned to drive so he walked four miles to work and back every day, with no complaint. He was instrumental in establishing a union at the steel mill at a time when union organizing was dangerous. My father told stories of the family having to hide in their house when union breakers would come looking for his Dad. My other grandfather, Papaw Leibee, not only worked full time at the steel mill, he also had a farm in the country where he raised cattle and crops. He built three houses in Westwood, just outside of Ashland, to accommodate his aging mother and his expanding family.

Papaw and Grandma Leibee

My father had nine siblings. He worked as a caddy at age 16 at the local country club to earn some money. The Blevins and Leibee households lived only a block apart so many of my aunts and uncles were high school friends and classmates. Westwood was a close-knit community where everyone knew their neighbors and children could play in most any yard. Having such a large extended family, I had family on almost every block when I was growing up.

Willie Blevins, the man who would become my father, served in the Korean War. He returned home to Ashland after his tour of duty ended in 1952. He started a new life of hard work to maintain an existence in Westwood in a neighborhood of working-class, blue-collar families. In his first year after his military stint, he worked ten different jobs on the riverboats on the Ohio River. Most of the employable men in Ashland were working at Armco or had railroad jobs. He was called to work at Armco during his second year out of the service, but was laid off when the Korean War ended. He then worked on the boats traveling the Great Lakes to deliver ore to steel mills. At some point he was called back to Ashland for a permanent position at Armco.

My father, Willie Blevins, during the Korean War with the dog he adopted while on base

While on a furlough from the military during the war, my father attended a neighborhood church ice cream social where he encountered my mother, "Pretty Polly." Willie and Pauline had dated in high school. Mom was a beauty and was never for a lack of dates or friends. She dated several boys, but it came down to two special suitors: my father and a boy named Russell. When Dad enlisted in the Army Air Force and was sent to Korea, the choice was made; she married Russell upon her high school graduation. Soon afterward, Polly had a baby.

At the time of that ice cream social, Polly was both a mother and a widow. Russell had suffered a cruel and painful death, burned and disfigured beyond recognition in a truck wreck. He lived seven days in agony and died on Mom's 20th birthday. I have been told that she sat by his bedside at the hospital the entire seven days, and, although his face was badly burned, she didn't hesitate to kiss him and try to comfort him. As he lay dying, they sang the song, Amazing Grace, together.

The meeting at the ice cream social must have rekindled some past feelings. My Dad asked his friend, Elwood Hall, to arrange a double date with the young widow. That date at the horse races in Cincinnati was the opportunity for Willie and Pauline to renew their relationship.

My mother was not only a woman of great beauty, but also a person of great strength. As a young girl she was given a lot of responsibility and often had to step in as caretaker for her younger siblings because my grandmother worked. I've always marveled at the courage she possessed as a widow and mother of an 18-month-old baby.

My parents were married in 1955 and at twenty-four, my dad was an instant father. Within a year they were planning for my arrival. My four-year-old half-sister, Patty, was eager to have a sister or brother, and my many aunts and uncles were eager for another addition to the family. I would be part of the first wave of grandchildren on both sides of the family. An assortment of cousins entered the family in waves of three or four at a time.

I was born on July 3, 1956. When my mother first started having labor pains at home, my father told her the story of the movie, "No Time for Sergeants," to relieve her discomfort until the pains got closer and they went to the hospital. The nurses there instructed my mother to hold back until the doctor arrived. After a long day of work at the hospital, he was napping. As my birth came closer and more difficult to suppress, the nurses went to find the doctor. As soon as he entered the room, I entered the world.

Immediately, the doctor noticed that I was turning blue around the mouth when I cried. The medical staff wasn't sure what was wrong with me. Nevertheless, I was sent home. My parents were frustrated, anxious, and scared knowing that something had happened during my birth. They were uncertain about the long-term effects. As my father later said, "Back then you did not question the doctors. You believed whatever they told you."

At a few weeks old, it was determined that I was having seizures. I was prescribed anti-seizure medications. The young family, already impacted by death, was faced with a disabled child. Little was known or understood about brain damage and birth defects at that time.

Me with my Dad

In the picture on the previous page, I think a lot must have been going on in my Dad's head, wondering why I was not developing as I should. I'm sure he was looking at me not only with love, but also with great apprehension.

My mother soon noticed I was not progressing as her first child did. I was not walking at the proper time. Instead, I would scoot using one hand. After seeing several doctors who could not correctly diagnose me, we went to see one of the best children's doctors in the area when I was 18 months old. As soon as my mother sat me on the exam table, the doctor took one look and declared, "she has cerebral palsy."

This was bittersweet for my parents. It was an enormous relief to find a doctor who could diagnose me, but a terrible blow to learn that their child was going to have life-long limitations. The next step for my parents was to find the best help available for a child with my issues. It was evident that I had little use of my left side, but more ramifications of my diagnosis would become obvious as I tried to walk and talk.

From the age of two, with the help of the enlightened pediatrician who diagnosed me, Dr. Guy Cunningham, I attended cerebral palsy clinics held at the local hospital. We would go and sit all day in a large room with other children and parents waiting to see specialists in orthopedic care and physical and speech therapy, and to learn more about cerebral palsy (CP). This trip was an all-day ordeal, beginning at sunrise and lasting until we had seen all the professionals I needed to see that day to evaluate my progress. It was often unpleasant and tiring for a child and I imagine it was for my parents, too. Looking back on it now, I would liken this experience to a cattle drive, with the children being herded from room to room. I would see people who wanted to measure me for leg braces or assess my improvement, if any, through speech and physical therapy. Although I knew it was necessary, I was always glad to leave.

At two and a half I was enrolled in a class for children with cerebral palsy and other physical challenges to learn to do the activities of daily living while also taking speech and physical therapy. The class was at Belafonte Hospital in Ashland. I remember having to dress and undress a doll repeatedly to learn to button up a shirt, zip up a pair of pants, and tie a shoe, all with one hand. There were several children in the class with a variety of limitations. Some children were in wheelchairs, some in full-body braces. This class served as a kind of test to see if we could attend regular public schools. I enjoyed going there because I could see other children like myself and we could share tricks on managing our challenges.

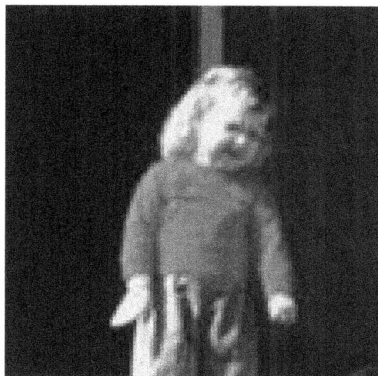

Most children begin their formal education in the first grade at the age of five or six. Some go to a kindergarten at four or five. However, few people share my extensive experience in the classroom setting. I started at the age of two and have continued to attend one type of class or another for the rest of my life. I guess that makes me a lifelong learner.

I met one of my first friends in those early classes. Her name was Paula McGlone. Once, we competed to be the local cerebral palsy poster child. The winner would have her photo used in some fundraising events for United Cerebral Palsy. She won and I always said it was because she was a blonde. Competition aside, we remained friends through high school. In fact, we are still friends to this day.

Paula and me then… and fifty years later.

Our teacher used a wheelchair, which was the first time I had ever seen anyone with a disability in a traditional job setting. I found out years later she committed suicide. This was a blow to me in several ways. My hope for a successful life was drained to doubt for a long time. Also, I was very fond of her and so sad to hear that the lady who greeted us with smiles each day was secretly facing despair to the point of taking her own life.

I'm pretty sure that having a child with a disability born into an already stressed, blended family had to be difficult for all involved. I have been told my father harbored guilt for my disability because Mom had one healthy child before I was born. The guilt added another layer of stress in our family because it seemed to my sisters that he loved me more than them. He was softer on me and it was obvious. It also caused tension around how I was to be raised.

My mother didn't treat me any differently than my sisters. I was allowed to take risks that my father would never have permitted. Had it been left to him I would have lived under his roof his entire life. Ultimately, he grew to see the wisdom of my mother allowing me to live as normal a life as possible. Shortly before his death, he told my mother how proud he was of her for the decisions she made regarding my upbringing.

There were countless hours spent on my frequent doctor appointments, searching for resources, and dealing with my delayed language, walking, and cognitive skills, which made it necessary for my mother to work with me daily on therapies to get me ready for mainstreaming into public school.

My older half-sister, Patty, had a lot more responsibility caring for me than any ordinary sister would. As we aged, time my parents should have been spent with Patty and her growing up had to be channeled to me. It was a good thing that Patty was an extraordinary child; she was strong, smart, and loving to all her sisters.

Patty played an important role in my learning to be social and learning to read by playing school with me. Since we shared a bed, it was easy to have my full attention. When she was ten and I was six, she read to me every night before sleep. We read the Bible most nights because our paternal grandfather was a preacher. I was assigned verses to memorize and repeat back to her later. She taught me to dress one-handed when it became necessary to add garments such as stockings and a bra.

Patty was and still is my hero.

My therapy continued as more children joined the family. My sister Teresa, who was born when I was three, viewed my therapy sessions as a game. She sat with Mom and me and actually learned to talk by repeating my exercises before I learned them. Teresa expertly mimicked phrases such as, "Little Lucy Lost Her Locket," and "Susie Sells Sea Shells by the Sea Shore."

By the time my sister Elizabeth was born when I was six, my parents were exhausted. It's a family joke that Elizabeth wasn't raised, she was jerked up. She was born with severe allergies and required regular medical visits and weekly shots. By this time, my parents were well schooled about the medical community and continued that routine until her high school years.

Although six years apart, Elizabeth and I were close as sisters and friends. To this day we understand and support each other, enjoy each other's company, and share an intimate relationship. She suffered a brain injury in recent years. Her recovery was a miracle and we often talk about it.

Elizabeth has said this about our family life:

"I feel very fortunate to have been raised in a family of all girls. Patty was a second Mom to me probably because Mom was so busy with everyone else and the farm. So I got plenty of attention until she went to college when I was 7.

"Having Tina as a sister trained me to be aware of other peoples' needs and help out when needed. As the baby, everyone else was already there so everything felt normal. Everyone was expected to contribute at their own highest level. We all had different likes and dislikes and skill sets. One thing I remember was thinking that my Mom's life was hard and that I wanted to be good and not make her cry. There was a lot going on in the house, family and marriage. I became somewhat of a loner or you might say an observer.

"Growing up in a very poor area, I saw lots of people with challenges. I learned how important family is to survival and the quality of life. Tina and I both had a giving heart and went into social work first, later branching out into civil rights and environmental issues."

Elizabeth goes on to say, "Having Tina as a sister was a reality check. I grew up knowing bad things happen to good people. Don't take things for granted and have gratitude for every blessing."

*   *   *   *

18

That's me on the left with my sisters,
Teresa, Elizabeth, and Patty

When I was learning to be mobile on my own strength I'd sit on the floor and pull myself from place to place with my good side. To any observers, it looked like I was working hard. My mother tells the story of when her sisters would visit and watch me strive to get to where I was going. My aunts would cringe and say, "How can you just sit there and let her struggle? I'm going to pick her up!"

"No," my mother would say, "she has to learn to do things herself."

This was how my mother taught me to face obstacles. Pretty soon I was able to pull myself up on furniture and take a few steps, clinging to a chair or table. I'd usually fall and look back at my audience with a grin on my face and then crawl back over to try again. This was the way I learned most things; I was left on my own to figure it out.

Developing and adapting ways to do tasks which normally require two hands has been an ongoing process for me. I'm immediately reminded of the Christmas I received my first tricycle when I was about five. No one was sure if I could manage riding it with one good hand and one leg in a heavy brace, but I was thrilled and eager to try.

The first attempt to get on and position my feet was successful and I began to pedal. The wheels started turning and I felt I had mastered it, but then realized I couldn't get the steering right. Since I didn't use my left hand, I automatically steered to the right. My starting point always led me straight into the corner of the kitchen and into a trash can over and over again. Then, finally, I got it. I took off through my chosen path and just before I arrived at the can for another blow, I took a sharp left, missed the can, and continued down the hall. I stopped and looked back to see everyone applauding my new skill. Dad was filming on an old 8mm camera and we've laughed at my determined ride many times since then.

My Dad always told me that when I was learning to ride a two-wheeled bike, I begged him to take off the training wheels long before he was comfortable with my ability to balance on two wheels only. Somehow, I convinced him that I was ready to ride without help. He walked with me up and down our little street in Westwood while I rode the bike, learning to control the steering and my balance. Apparently, neighbors along the street watched us as we made pass after pass by their houses. On one occasion, one neighbor, Mrs. McKenzie, stepped out and told Dad, "I'm really pulling for Tina to learn to ride that bike!" It helped having some cheerleaders in my corner.

My Mom and me

Chapter 2
"How fast can you run
in that thing?"

All the time I was attending special classes and seeing doctors, my parents were doing their own research on every available resource that might be of benefit to me. The 1950s offered little help for parents of a child with a disability. My father learned that California was one of the few states that offered free special education in public schools. He made an effort to find employment there, going as far as preparing a résumé and sending queries to several companies in the state. But by the age of four, it was evident to all that I did not require special education and could attend regular kindergarten. My parents abandoned their plans for a cross country move to begin the long journey of hunting and finding resources in our area.

In the classroom at Bellafonte Hospital, everyone was pleased with my progress. I graduated to a kindergarten class the next year and was transferred – we called it "mainstreamed" - into a class of "normal" children at four. I suspect this was a test to see if I'd be able to handle a public-school setting in the first grade.

I remember that year in kindergarten clearly for many reasons. Three stand out in particular: I had my first acting job, playing the Fat Lady in a circus; the teacher had a big, lovable Basset Hound; and it was the first time a boy gave me a ring.

We staged a circus for our parents. I was hoping to be the tightrope walker, but our teacher chose someone else. I was picked to play the Fat Lady. My mom outfitted me in a larger dress, stuffing it with rags to make me appear bigger. I had a skit that involved me pushing around a baby carriage, then stopping and talking lovingly to the contents of it. I then stooped to lift out what everyone thinks is going to be a baby but turns out to be a carriage full of snack food. Nowadays, that skit wouldn't exactly be politically correct.

My kindergarten was in the basement of my teacher's home. Her Basset Hound was named Mrs. Murphy. She kept us company on the playground and greeted us each morning with a wagging tail.

And now for the ring. On one occasion, a boy brought a Three Stooges ring to class from his father's corner variety store. It was three dimensional in that you could move it different ways and see the face of each stooge according to the position of the ring. He called me up front and presented me with the ring saying, "I would like Tina to have this ring." That would be the highlight of my romantic life for a long, long time!

None of my classmates had any physical limitations, but my teacher made me feel like I was no different from the others. She encouraged us all to do creative and independent activities. One such activity was Show and Tell, when each of us would prepare a short presentation on something of interest to us. I remember talking to the class on a few occasions about the farm that my father had bought. We would spend summers and weekends there while my father worked on the house, getting it ready for the family to move there permanently.

I attended first through third grades at the Renfroe Elementary School in Westwood, Kentucky. When I enrolled in the first grade, this big school situation might have been scary, but I had a large network of friends and family in the school. Many cousins close to my age attended the school and my grandmother was the school cook who I would see at lunchtime. She liked to tell the story of me coming through the line and carrying my tray by myself to the table, refusing assistance from the teacher's aide and others, saying "I can do it myself." She told my mother how proud she was of me for not letting others do what I could do for myself. It made her laugh to see me brush off help. I was happy attending this city school for the three years that I did. My neighborhood was filled with cousins and both sets of grandparents lived a block from me.

Here I am at a Christmas celebration with a group of cousins. I am at the far right in the third row from the bottom.

I have very special, happy memories of walking to school with my older sister or my mother's two younger sisters, Judy and Linda, who were in high school at the time. On those days when my aunts accompanied us, Patty and I would walk to my grandmother's house to meet up with them. We would watch them put on their makeup and fix their hair. By then, the milk man would have come by and left a fresh bottle of chocolate milk. Before leaving for school, we'd drink a glass of ice-cold chocolate milk. That was something we never got at home because we used a powdered chocolate mix. It was never as good as the already mixed, smooth milk from the milk man.

The walk home from school was usually just Patty and me, as my aunts preferred to be with their friends. We had an unusual short cut that went through a cemetery, which was frequently used by children in our neighborhood. This was never a spooky experience since many of our family members were laid to rest there and we were accustomed to visiting it with our parents.

We encountered other interesting places on the way home. I made a regular stop at a small corner store to buy red licorice to munch on as we walked. Patty and I made the acquaintance of a blind cobbler (shoe repairman) who lived in a place on our way home. His name was Bob White and occasionally we'd visit with him for a while. His home was filled with many interesting things for children. He showed us his Braille phone and phonebook. He read to us from his Braille Bible and let us feel the bumps that only he could understand.

My aunts Judy and Linda would come to play a large role in our lives as they were two of several babysitters we had. It was a real treat to have them there on a Saturday morning, because we'd all watch American Bandstand (a popular television show among teenagers of the time featuring current popular music) and Patty and I would observe as they practiced the latest dances. Sometimes my father's sister, Cora, came since she was friends with Judy and Linda. We'd all dance around the living room to the new songs that Dick Clark (the show's emcee) would introduce.

In the summer after my third grade, my father moved the family to the farm in the country, away from everything I loved. The change from an urban school to a rural school was drastic for me. I rode a bus for over an hour to school and back. The classes were small. My classroom included fourth and fifth grades. I was able to make friends with the children who lived near our farm by socializing on the school bus every day.

On my first day at the little country school a boy asked me, "how fast can you run in that thing?" as he pointed at my leg brace. I looked at him and sneered, "you want to find out?" I was pleased that he acknowledged the brace and had questions about it, instead of just staring and ignoring me. I was also amused because he didn't know I could go pretty fast in my own way.

Growing up with limited use of one side of my body, I had to be creative in doing everyday tasks such as dressing and chores like mowing the grass and laundering clothes on the old ringer washer and then hanging them on the clothesline with my one good hand. Putting hosiery and bras on presented special challenges.

But I am most proud of how I taught myself to run so I could keep up with my sisters and friends playing games. My leg brace came up to my knee which made it significantly more difficult to gain the balance and strength needed to do much more than walk. Living on a farm with a flat dirt road gave me the perfect place to practice. I'd walk as fast as I could from the house to the barn over and over. Gradually, I developed a kind of half run and half trot. Because one leg was shorter than the other, it was hard to get a smooth run. So, I'd do my trot run between the barn and the house and I improved to the point where I was able to run laps around the football field in high school with my Physical Education class. My teacher wanted to give me a pass on running, but I was determined to try it. She let me be part of the basketball games during class as a ball jumper.

The boy and I did race that day in the fourth grade on the playground. And he did beat me. However, it was the inclusion the race signified that I was hoping to find at my new school.

The next year I transferred to the grade school in town because my parents felt it offered a better education. This meant another thirty minutes longer each way on the school bus. I missed the intimacy of the small, rural school. In the school in town, there seemed to be social divisions among the students. This move proved to be my hardest adjustment. My leg brace made me stand out from the other students and I really felt my difference.

My new school was in Louisa, Kentucky. Louisa sits where the Levisa and Tug Forks come together, forming the Big Sandy River. The Big Sandy serves as part of the border between Kentucky and West Virginia. The town was established in 1822 and incorporated in 1869.

The Louisa-Fort Gay Bridge now spans the Levisa Fork and Tug Fork and connects Louisa, Kentucky, to Fort Gay, West Virginia. This bridge is a functional pedestrian crossing and a historical landmark. It is one of the few bridges in the world that connects two states while spanning two rivers.

Louisa is also notable for being the site of the first needle dam in the United States, completed in 1896 on the Big Sandy River. Such a dam is meant to control the level and flow of water through the use of 'needles' leaning against a solid frame. This innovation improved river navigation and transportation.

Music and church have formed a strong bond among its residents. Musicians are influenced by the bluegrass roots of the area's Irish and Scottish roots and old Baptist spirituals. Highway 23 that runs through Louisa is commonly known today as the Country Music Highway because of the number of country music stars that were born and raised along the route.

Chapter 3
On the Farm

My father was not an experienced farmer, but neighbors with homegrown expertise did not hesitate to teach him the proper way to tend the soil for the best garden or how to care for a herd of cattle. In return, my father would teach these government-shy farmers how to apply for grants to improve their farms. Years later I learned that each Thanksgiving he would buy baskets of food and turkeys and delivered them to homes in the community which he felt needed a little help. Nothing was said but, "thank you so much" by the recipients. We all lived thirty miles from town, so the people become dependent on each other, which enabled me to witness a community full of teachers and mentors.

A woman named Syrilda was our nearest neighbor. She was the strongest woman I have ever known. She ran a cattle farm single handed, working dawn to dusk, but she always had time to chat and make tasty pastries for hungry children as we got off the school bus. She became our second mother. It was the first time I had encountered such a strong, independent woman.

She enthusiastically encouraged me as I learned to do things on my own like riding a two-wheeled bike with one hand. My practice route ran past her house and since I was far from mastery, every trip ended with me landing in her rose bushes. She would pick me up and dust me off and give me a fresh homemade donut to soothe my tarnished ego. She put me back on my bike to return home saying, "you can do this!" Eventually I would ride for miles on the country roads. My bike became my ticket to freedom. I lived miles from my friends, but this little beauty would take me to see them. We would meet up and ride all day.

This was the bike I would ride for miles to visit friends in the country. I learned to ride on graveled roads.

One of the big things that I noticed was the poverty of the people in my community. It opened my eyes to just how much my family was blessed. I loved spending the night with friends. I got used to cooking a pot of beans on a pot belly wood stove that also served as the winter heat. Many nights we piled in bed with five kids and quilts piled so thick you could not move all night. Some friends did not have an indoor restroom, which meant a trek to the outhouse when needed.

Our farm became somewhat like camp for our city cousins. Each summer we would host several visitors who'd spend a few days with us. Our place held many attractions for children. There were hills, ponds, wildlife, and games to play with the two boys who lived on the next farm.

At family reunions now, whenever cousins reminisce about summers on the farm, someone will always want to talk about "Uncle Bob." Bob was an uncle of our friends on the next farm who would visit during the summer months. He was an elderly man, but ageless to children. He was totally blind. We heralded his return each year with celebration and glee. He brought joy to every child he met and he always had a riddle and a story. We'd play horseshoes and word games, pick up walnuts, or just talk until dark.

Bob was a champion nutcracker. He could sit for hours cracking our gathered walnuts and then pass out those yummy nuggets to each of us. Fun with Bob was different than with other adults. He understood kids and we knew it. We accepted him unconditionally, as he did us.

We learned to do things Bob's way. To play horseshoes, we would tap the stake with a metal pipe. Bob would hone in on the sound of the tapping and eight out of ten times he would make a ringer. When going for walks in the holler, he used a walking stick or would hold the hands of two delighted children.

When I was ten, sitting on the porch of the old farmhouse one day, Uncle Bob said to me, "Someday you will get too old to come see old Bob. You'll grow up and have other friends to see and that will be ok."

"No," I protested, "I'll never do that to you, Bob."

Sadly, he was right. Children grow up and have other interests. Bob died when I was 25. I realized that I didn't even know where he lived or what his home life was like during the rest of the year. We only knew that when Bob came to the holler, it was lots of fun. I felt like I had let him down and it broke my heart.

Bob was a simple man who taught us a simple message, which he lived every day: Love and respect your children, your family, and yourself; allow for differences; and you can love and be loved.

When I was growing up on the farm, we always kept an outdoor dog to protect the property and keep us company. Each dog had his or her own personality. Barky was an old grouch. Spicket was maternal. Sugarfoot had an independent nature and often disappeared for days. Elky was a real class act who kept her coat neat, never ate while being watched, and never chased cats or cars. Then there was Shadow. Shadow wandered onto the farm and into our hearts. Shadow was the dog who taught me that the value of a dog is not necessarily related to beauty or intelligence.

Shadow came to us in the manner in which we usually acquired dogs. He showed up at the back door hungry and lost. He was just a pup, but his huge paws gave evidence that he would be an enormous dog one day. These paws were to later plow through my mother's flowerbeds and trample me to the ground while innocently trying to show me affection.

Two of Shadow's more amusing features were his gawky looks and his simpleton nature. He was a large, black figure with a huge head. I always got a chuckle when I saw him gallop up the lane with his long ears flopping and flying in the wind. I don't like to say that he was dumb because I loved him. But he just couldn't seem to understand his purpose was to protect. He allowed deer to eat the vegetable garden and flowers and only barked when family and neighbors arrived at the house. When strangers come on the property, Shadow greeted them with a wagging tail and a friendly nudge on the leg as he begged for petting.

And Shadow was exceptionally good at begging. He begged for attention, for affection, and especially for food. He had a very effective whine; when he started to sing his long, soulful tune, you might think he hadn't been fed for days. After being fed by one person, he would come to me with that mournful tune and I would fall for his starving dog act, tricked into feeding him a second time.

Shadow was a loyal dog. When I lived in another state and returned home for visits, Shadow seemed to know my car. He ran to meet me at the end of our long drive and paced alongside my car, which was about the same size as him. As I opened my door, I would instantly get a huge, black head blocking my exit. Once I got past that obstacle, he'd stand in my path and flop down his big, slobbering, whiny face in my lap for a petting. It truly made me feel as though I'd been missed, and that I meant something special to him.

Shadow was always eager to go for walks with me. If he saw me start to leave the yard, he would take his place at my side. We strolled along until he grew bored with my slow pace. On the return trip, he usually would disappear about halfway home. But no matter how far we walked, the routine was the same. As I reached the drive, I would find Shadow spread out over the front yard fast asleep. You'd think he just finished a thirty-mile hike.

Shadow wasn't the brightest dog, and his looks weren't blue ribbon, but he was full of life, love, and loyalty. He was my walking companion, and always made me laugh with his puppy ways. He greeted me with so much joy that I found it impossible not to love this big, black, smelly lump of a dog.

Of all the dogs I've owned, Shadow was the most helpless. He wouldn't know how to get food if we didn't serve it to it him in a bowl and he wouldn't venture far from home without human accompaniment. But he was the one who most needed a loving home and we needed his simple, sweet, comic antics for our daily laughs.

Chapter 4
"No, You Just Can't Do That"

Me in high school

In the fall of 1970, I entered Louisa High School. My time in high school would prove to be lonely, isolating, and depressing. As a teenager with little self-confidence, I was terribly unhappy. Being physically different, painfully shy, and plain looking, I did not make friends easily. My acquaintances were other oddball characters in the school. There was the overweight person; the girl who once dated the whole football team, at one time; the boy suspected of being gay; the girl who was so poor she wore the same two dresses each week; and the girl with cerebral palsy and the funny walk. That, of course, was me.

We were not a collective group; I knew each one separately. Individually we all had our own pain and sometimes we'd show a little understanding to each other in our own way. We were the little, dateless bunch at the table in the back on prom night. We weren't really friends with each either, we just knew that we were in similar situations. Pain and loneliness are strong bonds, even if shared from a distance.

I failed to take a grip and make the best of my time in high school. I see now, because of immaturity, I spent a lot of time in self-pity and bitterness. I received little encouragement from the school staff at a time when I was searching for direction and vocational help. It would take many years and many more failures to learn to accept myself.

As I sit here writing this now in my sixties, I can name a hundred things that I wanted to do with my life. I wanted to be a librarian, a disability advocate, a writer, a teacher, or a songwriter. I wanted to help create an open and inclusive world. If you had asked me at 17 what I was going become, I could not answer that question because I was so unsure of my abilities. I received no counseling on what the options were open to me.

I remember my older sister knew from an early age that she wanted to be a pharmacist. My Dad took her to meet with a local pharmacist. I felt lost with no direction. That is one of the downfalls of public schools then. At that time, they did not give disabled students any vision of the future beyond high school.

At one time I thought I could possibly be a librarian since I loved books. I had noticed that students worked in the school library during study hall. Thinking it would be a good opportunity to try out that vocation, I approached the school librarian.

"Mrs. Smith, how does a student get a job in here during study hall?" I asked, in an unusually bold move for me.

"You can't do it," she replied. "You have to go through the superintendent, and you can't."

"But I know the system. I can find and file books," I offered, hoping to break her stern look.

"No, you just can't do it," she answered, in a way meant to finish the conversation, and walked away.

I've often wondered if I had been given that opportunity and was able to gain a little confidence in my abilities, it might have changed the direction of my life. I might still be happy in the stacks of some library, never having to experience the stress and strife that put me where I am today, with numerous other challenges.

I have always envied people who knew at an early age what they wanted to do with their lives. This was not the case for me. There were too many unknowns in my life, like how long I would live, or whether I'd be able to work. The realization of what I wanted to do came to me very gradually, as the people in my life - from childhood and as I aged - began to influence how I would view my abilities and identify my passions. They would eventually color my world with possibilities. The first came from listening to stories of how my grandfather worked at his great peril to help form a union at the local steel mill.

I was taught early to stand up and right the wrongs of society from my family of blue-collar steel workers who were actively establishing unions and confronting management. My grandmother talked about times when my grandfather's life was in danger when organizing unions in the 1930s. She and her children learned to hide from the thugs sent by management. My father was also a union organizer. He grew to be an effective advocate, negotiating many times for his fellow laborers in disagreements with management. Later, he dabbled in politics and came to know many influential people in the community and in Kentucky as a whole. He was to teach me many lessons in civic involvement though much of what he did was not known to me until later in life.

One thing I definitely learned from my father was that education was the important key to achieving one's goals. He told all of us that we must attend one year of college then we were on our own. He made me believe college was an option and made sure I went to a nearby university after high school. By the time I graduated high school I was ready to tread new waters as a freshman at Morehead State University. Morehead State was a public university with about 4,000 students at the time. It was about 60 miles from my home. My first attempt at college, however, was not successful. I didn't take the educational opportunity seriously. At seventeen, away from home for the first time, I viewed it as more of a social occasion, and was carefree and careless. It ended with me returning home. I had reluctantly enrolled in college and flunked out after one year. I moved back home feeling even more lost in 1975.

It was at this time, I became aware of vocational rehabilitation services when a friend suggested I meet with Wade Bailey, the local field counselor for the Kentucky Bureau (now Office) of Vocational Rehabilitation. Vocational rehabilitation, a state-federal program, can be traced back to the aftermath of World War I. It was created to support injured veterans returning to civilian life. In the United States, this led to the passage of the Smith-Hughes Act (1917) which laid the groundwork for vocational education. However, the real turning point came with the Smith-Fess Act of 1920, often referred to as the "Civilian Vocational Rehabilitation Act." This landmark legislation extended vocational rehabilitation services beyond veterans, offering assistance to civilians with disabilities for the first time. Voc Rehab, as it is commonly called, is intended to provide individuals with disabilities the training and other services they need to go to work and become tax-paying citizens.

Vocational rehabilitation has played a crucial role in shaping employment opportunities for individuals with disabilities, evolving alongside societal attitudes and legislative advancements. The history of vocational rehabilitation is deeply intertwined with broader movements for disability rights and workforce inclusion.

Taking my friend's advice, I met with Mr. Bailey. He said something significant to an unsure, worried teenager looking for answers and eased the anxiety about the future.

He said that one bad year of college at 17 did not make me less intelligent and that many young people are not ready for college directly after leaving high school. He explained there were alternative ways to accomplish my employment goals, such as vocational training. Shortly thereafter, I entered the Carl D. Perkins Comprehensive Rehabilitation Center in Thelma for evaluation. In addition to evaluation. The center also provided job skills training. Thelma was about 30 miles from Louisa.

The two-week evaluation process at the Perkins Center tested not only my intelligence, physical abilities, and social skills but also my ability to form a serious life goal and commit to accomplishing it. While at the center, I gained the skills and confidence to concentrate my efforts toward an employment goal and overcome individual limitations to find a lifestyle that would give me the greatest satisfaction. You will never guess the conclusion from all my evaluations—go back to college!

This time, I had the support of the Center staff and a more mature outlook on post-secondary learning. I lived at the center and attended classes at nearby Prestonsburg Community College. This small college offered more guidance to the students and gave me the chance to get involved in more activities related to the classes. I did better there and it helped me rebuild my confidence. With a new attitude, I transferred to Northern Kentucky University (NKU), a public state university in suburban Cincinnati, to finish my Social Work Degree.

While at NKU in the 70's I had a teacher, Tony Mazzero, who was a very giving person. Tony was the director of the Social Work Department at NKU at the time. He was the first adult male I had ever met who felt strongly about equal rights and women's ability in society. He worked with me on my low self-esteem by giving me important assignments. He even filmed me during one exercise, so I was forced to see myself as an attractive person, something I never believed was true. I did not encounter men like him in my rural Eastern Kentucky town so it was a powerful lesson on the possibility of doing great things as a disabled woman and as a social worker.

Tucked away deep in one of my closets is an old wooden folding chair that I acquired more than thirty years ago. The paint is chipped from most of it, but it still provides a strong foundation, much like the lesson I learned the summer it was given to me.

I was a 19-year-old country girl fresh off the farm attending college in Northern Kentucky. It was my first real independent living experience, and I was feeling insecure. I got a job at the Sisters of the Good Shepherd Convent taking care of elderly nuns, providing intimate care for eighteen fragile women on the midnight shift. I lived in their boarding house for girls and stayed nights at the convent, watching over them. We would talk during the night and they grew to trust me and my presence in what I'm sure was a very personal space for them. They would tell me how safe they felt when I was on duty Their affection and confidence in me were empowering.

I would sit up through the night alone in what seemed to me to be a castle, listening for signs of distress from the sisters' rooms. When the morning came and all was well with my little group, I was thankful for another calm night. My actual reward came as I dressed the ladies for the day. Each one had their own special needs. Their habits consisted of layers of stockings, slips, and dresses, and it required care and effort to dress each one in their appropriate garb. Sister Rose, in particular, took more nurturing and time. After I put on her gown, glasses, earphone, and false teeth and combed her hair, she looked at me, smiled and said, "I love you."

My self-esteem grew during those nights chatting with the sisters. I grew close to the house mother, Sister Anne. I will never forget their enormous trust and belief in me.

By the end of the summer, the job and the sisters had given me confidence in my own abilities. As a token of their love, I was taken to the attic of the enormous convent and allowed to pick from the old furniture stored there to furnish my first apartment. Among the items I chose were my four "nun chairs." These chairs are still in use today for family gatherings. It still makes me smile when I see one.

I found the larger campus at Northern Kentucky University to be a successful experience. Empowered by the positive experience I'd had my year at Prestonsburg Community College, I appreciated the opportunity that lay before me. After three years, I graduated with my degree in Social Work in 1978 and was certain that I'd never need to go to school again. Little did I know.

I immediately went to work after graduation. After working in my field for some time, I was hired at a Louisa nursing home doing intake. I had achieved my dream. At twenty-two, my independent life was really happening!

Chapter 5
A California Adventure

I will never know why I did what I did next, but I quit my job after a year and moved to California to be with my best friend who was already living there. I was still searching for acceptance and inclusion and I thought California could give it to me. I had grown up secretly wanting to move to San Francisco and live the Bohemian lifestyle in a commune. I didn't have faith in my ability to live independently and this chance was too enticing to pass up. The lesson I learned in California is that you can move across the country, but all your problems tuck themselves into your suitcase and show back up when you unpack. On top of that, it became clear that I had missed the revolution by about ten years.

As far back as I can remember in my adolescence, I dreamed of going to a place where minds were open to differences. I wrote to a couple of communes in high school looking for a place where I could work with other people to have a home, a living, a purpose, friends, and live without judgement. It was the hay day of the hippie movement and California was the place to go. My life in a small town was limiting. I longed to be free. Those were the thoughts I had as I quit my job in Louisa and moved with a friend who had lived in California for couple of years. She had come home for a visit and talked me into dropping everything in Louisa and going back with her. She was successful in auto sales. She was also disabled, from polio, and faced her own rejections in small town life and had her own reasons to seek inclusive, accessible living. She told me California was where I needed to go.

What I did not realize was all my insecurities, low self-esteem, and poor body image did not stay in Kentucky. They got off the plane with me at LAX. But doors did open for me. I learned to live independently in Southern California, although I had to work 50 hours a week to keep financially viable. This was a huge step for this girl from the 'holler'; learning bus routes, going to the beach alone, learning to speak Spanish, meeting people from many cultures, and working in a shoe store.

For the full story on my California sojourn, we have to go back to 4th grade. I just moved from the Ashland school full of cousins to this country school at the start of the school year. I knew no one and had to ride the school bus for a long time to get there. I was still wearing a foot brace up to my knee on my left leg which made me even more awkward in my new school. On my first day I was in the restroom and saw another girl with the same kind of brace. I was too shy to talk to her but on the bus ride home, I was so excited to tell my sister what I saw in the bathroom. Another girl sitting nearby said, "that's my sister Brenda, she has polio." Brenda and I became fast friends on the long bus rides home, went bike riding, spent weekends together until we graduated from high school.

She was two years older than me so she tried college while I struggled to find my future. She ended up moving to California. I ended up going to the Perkins Center after flunking out of Morehead. I was not ready for college life. In the meantime, Brenda was building a successful life in car sales. I went on to graduate college and was working at a nursing home.

During a visit home she talked me into going back to California with her. It was a lifelong dream of mine. It did not take much convincing for me to go. Brenda lived in Santa Ana in Orange County just south of Anaheim and 33 miles southwest of Los Angeles. I moved in with her, her daughter, Summer, and her partner, Larry. We split up responsibilities and I helped with childcare.

I did not have a car so job hunting was hard. I found out to get a decent job in social work in California, I needed a master's degree. That was not possible. I found a job at a

41

shoe store in a shopping plaza within walking distance from the house. I sold shoes. I really enjoyed talking to customers, finding special shoes. I had a lot of repeat customers. I learned to speak Spanish because most of my customers were Mexican. My manager liked me and there was talk of management, but I just wanted a job with no real responsibility.

There was one group of customers I had at the store because none of the other salespeople wanted to interact with them. It was drag queens. Large women shoes were hard to find but I made sure we had a selection of colors and large sizes. They would have balls to dress for and I asked them what color their dresses were and go from there. My manager didn't mind because they spread the word and he sold a lot of shoes.

Meanwhile, Brenda's partner was getting restrictive about what I could do. His house, whatever. He did not like my dates coming there. A co-worker and I had already discussed sharing expenses on an apartment. We found a nice two-bed, one bath on the bus route. What I did not know was she planned to move her boyfriend in, too. I made it work. I was working 50-hour weeks to afford the apartment, food, bus fare, and trips to the beach or movies by us on days off.

Her boyfriend had his buddies coming and going, too. One of them asked me out. I did not have a car so I took him up on the offer. One day he took me on a drive around Southern California. We drove to San Diego to a high-rise office building. I waited in the car and he came back with a pouch. We then drove back to Santa Anna to a storage unit where he opened the door. I could see it was full of filing cabinets and what looked like junk. He came back and said, "I gotta clean that out sometime." I said I would help him. He just snickered.

When we got back to the apartment he laughed when he told my roommate's boyfriend, "Hey, Tina wants to help clean out the storage unit." They both laughed. Now, I felt uneasy thinking they were drug runners. One night later my "date" told me his contact in San Diego dealt with stolen diamonds and he and his friends would fence them.

Not long after that my roommate wanted me to go to her doctor with her. I went and the doctor and she tried to get me to swear that I witnessed my friend falling at work so she could sue her employer. I could not afford to live alone and did not want to move back to Brenda's house. I was missing my family very much after missing one Christmas in Kentucky. I decided to move home. Brenda tried and tried to get me to stay, even taking me to her psychiatrist. It did not work.

I understood why Brenda stayed. She had grown up with an abusive father who beat his children, cheated on her Mom openly, and had children with other women. She made her own loving family in California. She owns a car service now and is doing very well. In recent years, I have lost her friendship over political differences. It made me very sad.

It was a time of personal growth for me, navigating the huge cities. I gained some confidence and worked at a shoe store. I took advantage of my high school Spanish. I rode buses to the beach on my days off. I walked to and from work, developing strength and balance. But the cost of living proved to be a challenge and I began to regret the move. I sorely missed Christmas with my family. So, I packed up all my anxiety and depression and headed back to Kentucky, not knowing my next step.

*   *   *   *

There was one funny thing that occurred while I was living in California: my Mom and her four sisters appeared on Family Feud. They were big fans of the show. They had discussed trying out for the show for a long time. They got picked to fly out for further interviews. You have to realize my Mom and her sisters were nice looking so they were easily chosen to play against other trial families who were also in LA to be on the show. I was living about forty miles north of LA in Santa Anna.

My Mom and her sisters on the game show Family Feud in the early eighties

The week they were in town everyone who saw these five attractive sisters knew why they were in town and asked when they were going to be on Family Feud. They went out to see the sights and were shocked to see men dressed as women, openly gay couples and one young man who had his nipples pierced with gold chains. This was in the late seventies. Southern California culture was drastically different from Eastern Kentucky culture. They saw a couple of sitcom stars and that was a thrill.

One night they walked down the street in Hollywood to find a place to eat. They saw a place that was nice and not too busy. They walked in and got seated at a table. As they were reading the menu, one by one they started looking around at the other patrons and slowly realized it was a lesbian restaurant. They just looked at each other and said, "well, we are here, food looks good. Let's just enjoy it."

The day they went to the studio for try outs they had no say who would be the head of family for the game. The producers picked my Aunt Carolyn who was loud and had a good stage presence, but had not really watched the show on a regular basis. So they went on as the Toney family, her married name. During the try outs they were winning every game. The staff were telling them they were going to win big!

I rode the bus from Santa Ana to Hollywood to be in the audience. I got to town and took a cab to the CBS studios. I didn't know it had a million gates and I ended up walking a mile to the Family Feud gate and got there just in time to get seated. My friend Kaycee met me there to watch the taping. I remember thinking how tiny the studio looked compared to seeing it on television. Both families came out to be introduced and cameras rolled. A couple of days before the show Richard Dawson had an accident and broke a few ribs so he was in severe pain, but he did his usual joking and giving each lady a kiss.

They were instructed before the real game to huddle and have everyone agree on an answer before saying it. Well, Carolyn who was deemed the head of the family ended up giving her own answer. Needless to say, they did not win. The other family, as it turns out, had put down four other families in a row. The Toney family came home with great memories and Mary Kay beauty products. I met them as they exited the back and all I could say was, "you guys looked great!" Richard gave Mom an extra kiss because she did not make it to speed round. It was a fun day.

Let's Play 'Family Feud'

What started as a family reunion last year, ended up as a trip to Hollywood and an appearance as contestants on ABC's "Family Feud." These five sisters, seated, from left, Pauline Blevins, Louisa; Judy Brown, Lexington; Carolyn Leibee Toney, Russell; Linda Davis, Brunswick, Ohio; and, standing, Janice Mansfield, Norfolk, Va., went armed with a commission of Kentucky Colonel for host Richard Dawson.

To be chosen as contestants, the sisters had to pass two interviews, and later learned that only 25 out of 1,500 people are selected to appear during one week's taping.

The sisters, who were also named Kentucky Colonels by Governor Julian Carroll, will be seen as the Toney Family on the show, which is scheduled for Monday, Sept. 10, at 11:30 a.m. on the network.

An article from the Ashland (Kentucky) Daily Independent newspaper.

Chapter 6
The Eighties

Back in Kentucky, I began job hunting and quickly found a social work position at the Mountain Comprehensive Care Center in Prestonsburg working with families with high-risk children. My job was to do needs assessments on infants with disabilities and refer the parents to the appropriate agencies for services like speech and physical therapy. It seemed that the job would be well suited for me, having grown up in the "system." However, I was not prepared emotionally nor was I mature enough or assertive enough to handle the doctors and other stakeholders to complete my job. The toll it took on my confidence and ego were huge. I soon felt overwhelmed covering five counties in rural Eastern Kentucky. My family home visits took me on some roads that were essentially dirt paths. I remember being very scared at times to knock on the doors of strangers. It didn't take long for me to develop physical and neurological impairments. It was my dream job to work with children with special needs in the rural areas of Kentucky and I was failing miserably.

I was living alone in a small apartment experiencing headaches and depression to the point of considering suicide. I even started packing up my apartment so my family wouldn't be burdened with that chore after I was gone. I was unkempt and began to miss work. I saw a doctor for depression and was prescribed an antidepressant, which caused seizures. While on the job, I experienced loss of memory and petit mal seizures which confused my mind. I remember not going to work because of severe headaches, laying on the floor of my tiny three-room apartment, curled up in a ball crying.

By the time I made the decision to quit that job, I was on the verge of a serious breakdown. I sobbed for days before I called my family. When my mother came to my apartment she said, "you look like you haven't slept or bathed in a week."

She took me to my office to tell them of my condition. When my boss saw me, he said, "My God, Tina, I had no idea you were this sick. You look like you just crawled out from under a bus." All I knew was that I could not continue working at a job that was stressing away the life from my body and spirit. Working with children who I desperately wanted to help but couldn't because I was not effective consumed my soul bit by bit.

It took months, living back with my parents, to recover from my illness on new medication. I desperately needed to find a way to be independent again and knew that meant returning to school.

After much self-examination, I enrolled at Eastern Kentucky University (EKU) in Richmond to work on a Medical Records Degree. I thought if I coupled my Social Work Degree with a Medical Records Degree, I could work in a hospital with medical records and still be in an environment to help people.

EKU was another large campus with many things to do. The fall semester in 1980 was full of promise and anticipation. Unfortunately, I would not enjoy it. If I had known of the unfortunate events that would conclude that school term, I would have returned to the security of my home. School was way too stressful and the stress would manifest itself in physical illness and seizures.

The semester commenced with great excitement for new challenges, a new community, and a promising future. However, a month into my schoolwork the headaches started. I attributed them to the increased reading, long study hours, and tension. But the headaches continued and I began to experience short-term memory loss. I was losing things or forgetting things like where I parked my car, something I might call "senior moments" now. I kept attending classes, even though the content of the lessons didn't stick with me.

I now believe that the event that may have caused these new problems occurred one day when I was doing laundry on the next floor down from my room in the dorm. I was carrying a basket of clothes down the steps like I had done many times. I lost my balance and tumbled down a flight of steps hitting my head very hard on the concrete floor. I did not pass out and I was still able to speak when the paramedics rushed me to the hospital. I saw the doctor and because I was talking coherently, he decided not to do any X-rays of my head. I remember him saying something about radiation exposure. I did not protest his decision. I was in my early twenties and I still was under the delusion that doctors knew best. Also, not much was known about brain injury, strokes, brain bleeds and seizures. I returned to campus and classes.

Within a week I developed two black eyes and my vision changed. I am now certain that I had suffered a brain bleed. It was then that I started having memory loss, etc. I look back and wonder if he had ordered the X-ray could I have been spared a life of hardships and grief. In retrospect, I should have asked for a first-floor room in the dorm, but I was too stubborn to do the easy thing. If people learn anything from reading this book, I hope it is that asking for the easy way is a sign of wisdom not weakness.

After the incident, I would lose my balance and I fell several times. I still tried to attend classes. By the end of the second month, my memory problems increased. I found myself in places without recalling how I got there. Living in a new community, the people around me didn't have a frame of reference to judge my condition; there was no one to alert me or my family of my deteriorating health. Any reasonable thinking person would have sought medical attention. But in my weakened mental and physical state, I did not know how badly I needed help. I was terribly confused.

The memory I have now of that time is patchy, though I do remember some things with a punishing clarity. I remember receiving a telephone call from a friend in another city. I thought, "Thank God, someone knows where I am!" I had begun to feel as though I was living in a time warp, and no one would ever find me. Yet, I still did not go for help.

Another haunting memory was when I went to a telephone booth to call my parents and, as I was standing in the booth with the phone in my hand, I realized that I had no idea how to use a telephone. I tried to reconstruct the steps to make the call - pick up the phone, put the coin in the slot, dial. The words went through my mind, but my brain couldn't grasp their meaning. Angry and frustrated, I sank to the bottom of the booth, sobbing and praying.

Somehow, I made it back to my room. My roommate called my parents, and they came for me the next day. I must have been a shocking sight to them. They took me to University of Kentucky Medical Center in Lexington for a neurological examination. During this dark period, I was also losing my speech in a gradual progression and the loss of peripheral vision in both eyes was making reading difficult and driving dangerous. Yet again, I had to return to my parents to recover and regroup.

The next few months after my departure from EKU were filled with doctors, exams, and medications. It is still a blurry, foggy part of my memory. Some doctors thought I probably had a stroke; some thought I suffered brain damage from one of the falls, but no new brain damage beyond my original CP scar could be detected on CT scans. I tell people now I had a stroke because I was never given a definitive cause.

It took almost two years to regain my strength and health. I never regained the ability to talk. The loss of my speech has been the hardest of my many disabilities to accept. It has isolated me in ways that are beyond words. One of my greatest joys in life has always been a spontaneous and enjoyable meeting of minds with new people. Losing my speech was more than losing an audible voice. I lost the exchange of listening and responding with timing, laughter, and rhythm.

The loss of speech feels like a slow erasure of identity. People who are nonverbal are underestimated. My conversations, once a source of joy, debate, and intimate exchanges have become a battleground of frustration and grief. People assume that I am less intelligent. That combined with my physical appearance can builds walls.

Recently, I asked my sister, Patty, what she remembered about this period of my life and she had a few more details. She says, "Since it is over 40 years, my memories are a bit vague now. You were doing social work and living alone, the job was stressful and you had episodes at night so we went to Dr Browning. It sounded like depression to him so he prescribed an anti-depressant. What he did not know, me either, was that you had seizures as a baby and antidepressants can lower seizure threshold actually increasing the risk of seizures. Your situation became worse so you left your job, moving home. Dr Browning switched you to phenobarbital for the seizure activity and we went to neurologists in Huntington (West Virginia) to see what was going on.

"Since your job was stressful, you quit and went to EKU to go in a different direction, but your health declined, you took a bad fall and moved back home. I noticed your speech was deteriorating. I could no longer understand you and you had more and more difficulty swallowing so we went to UK for another opinion. You went through visual screening and I could see that you had lost part of your field of vision, which could lead to falls. You even saw the neurologist who did David's brain surgery and he could not see the reason, but mentioned the possibility of pseudobulbar palsy which could be progressive and fatal. Some of the doctors questioned Mom and asked if anyone outside our family had ever understood your speech and I told them your speech professor in college could understand her speech. I realized they thought you had always been non-verbal and we were looking for a miracle. Some doctors seem to think shouting at you could help and you would look at me and Mom like what was their problem.

"After trying and failing to get answers, we all felt that you would just have to move forward. You decided to call it a stroke. I felt that maybe the new incident was in the same area as the cerebral palsy and therefore was not seen. Perhaps you are right that the fall at EKU caused a brain bleed that led to the change of symptoms and the ultimate loss of speech and swallowing."

It would take years of aspiration and pneumonia to convince me to stop trying to eat and begin feeding myself through a tube in my stomach.

My sister Elizabeth, then a freshman at Morehead State University, invited me to live with her and try a couple of classes to test my capacity to handle structured learning. I took classes in one hand typing and nonverbal communication and did well. That gave me the courage to look to the future. If I could handle class work, I believed that I could learn to do a job. I didn't know what kind of job, but I knew it would mean more schooling.

Again, I looked for guidance from vocational rehabilitation and returned to the job training center in Thelma to take courses in computer operations and business office administration. I lived at the center for two years to complete the course. The educational setting there was much different than any I had experienced previously. The classes were geared to accommodate those with disabilities. The learning pace was set by the student. Everyone there was trying to overcome their limitations. It was a good time to evaluate my abilities and set new goals. There was no feeling of being different and successes were enthusiastically celebrated.

When I entered the job training/rehabilitation center in 1981, I had no means of communication other than a rather heavy speech device with a male voice. It took a lot of patience to have a conversation.

The center was filled with people of differing abilities and backgrounds. However, I was most drawn to the deaf students. I did not know sign language at the time, but I knew I needed to learn it to broaden the ways in which I could communicate and be able to make new friends. My roommate, Karen, was deaf so that even further motivated me to learn the language.

There was also a deaf man, Russell, at the center who I found to be pleasant company. I asked him to teach me to sign and he agreed. Every evening after dinner we would meet in the empty cafeteria for our lessons. He was very patient with me and taught me many signs I could do with one hand. I could then go to my room and practice my new skill with my roommate.

I learned fast and was soon conversing with the deaf students along with the hearing students who knew some signs. When new students enrolled in the center and saw the frequent use of sign, some would ask me to teach them. I was more approachable because I could hear. The new students often came in feeling scared and lonely away from their family often for the first time and wanted to find ways to be included. On several occasions, a young man was attracted to a deaf girl and wanted to be able to communicate with her. Often it was a good excuse for long walks to escape the center for a while and do sign as we walked.

After completing the vocational course in Office Management in 1985, I started searching for a job. I was not confident I would find one. I moved in with a friend in Northern Kentucky and began to send out resumes and go on interviews. This was the area where I had attended college years before and I enjoyed the area very much. It offered cultural events, such as music, art, and lectures. My reception during interviews was usually not enthusiastic due to doubts about my ability. I soon recognized the "look" that meant I had no chance. After three months of rejection, a friend who was also disabled referred me to a supported employment agency that would sponsor me for six months by paying my salary as a trial period. They would also provide me with individualized supports on the job once I started. The agency arranged an interview at AT&T in Cincinnati, Ohio. I started working as a temporary data processing clerk for a group of engineers working to transfer phone wires from analog to digital. I received no benefits or any promise of being hired. I faced opposition from a few of the supervisors.

My interaction with my co-workers, though, was encouraging and fun. They were patient with my communication device and eager to know me. I met a co-worker who knew sign language and she became a mentor to me. She invited me to join the Toastmasters Club, a local chapter of Toastmasters International. This nonprofit educational organization helps people improve their public speaking, communication, and leadership skills through structured practice and peer feedback. I became its only mute member. I would do my speeches in sign language, and my friend interpreted them.

During my years at AT&T, I taught sign language to my coworkers, went to lunch with colleagues, was hired with full benefits, and was invited to social events. At this time, I was having difficulty eating, making it messy and slow. I did not accept invitations to go eat with co-workers when my supervisor took the team out. After a few times of ducking invitations, they assured me they did not care about how I ate, they just wanted me to go with them. The first time was hard to do. I used many napkins and coughed a few times. But I received nothing but encouragement from the team, maybe because my boss lengthened our lunch break to accommodate me. I enjoyed many lunches out with co-workers. It was a gesture of understanding and inclusion I will never forget.

My office was located in a 30-story office building on the corner of Fourth and Main in downtown Cincinnati. On certain days, if the wind blew hard, it would gust around the corner of the building with a terrific force. Each day I had to cross the street to get to my bus stop. On some days, the wind would blow with such a force that it nearly knocked me off balance and into the traffic. On one occasion, I was in such a bluster it forced me to cling to a newspaper-vending box to keep from tumbling into the street. I had visions of Mary Poppins floating up, up and away.

One calm day, I stood on the corner and looked to the other side. It did not look to be a far walk, but in the midst of high winds it seemed like miles. I crossed the street and counted my steps. There were 15 steps. Now, I knew it was not miles and miles. It was just 15 steps!

I still had to deal with the windy days and all other anxiety filled situations. I started to think about the strength and courage I would need to meet this "challenge." Where could I go to find strength in all situations? Where could I get the strength of armies and the courage of warriors? I began to pray about this problem. It did not take long to get inspired. What I literally needed was the bulk of an elephant to steady me in the gusting winds. So, the next windy day as I approached the corner, I said a little prayer. As I made my first step, in my mind I became the giant gray beast. From the first moment, I felt the heaviness of my steps. I made the steps one by one doing the "elephant walk" with a confidence and assurance that I'll always make it to the fifteenth step safely to the other side.

I have used the "elephant walk" many times in my life in many other fearful situations. I keep a little elephant toy in sight to remind myself that inside this little lady is a huge, fearless mass of strength and courage I can call on to help me face anything.

I worked at AT&T for five years. I loved that job. It was a data entry job and had none of the stress I had encountered as a social worker. I had a 9:00 to 5:00 schedule and could go home with a clear head. The Internet had just come out and I was trained on the world wide web. I was hoping to retire from

AT&T. Unfortunately, when the country's recession began, AT&T started to downsize. My supervisor advised me to save money because the company planned a massive layoff in two years. Thanks to his advice, by the time I was laid off, I had enough resources to live for two years while I went to college. As part of my separation package, AT&T paid for two years of college classes. At age 35, I realized my next decision would have to be one that could secure my future for a lifetime.

Me with my co-workers at AT&T

In the picture above, I am with some of my co-workers at AT&T. The woman on the right in the photograph was one of the supervisors who recommended I be hired out right. She treated me very well during my time there.

The woman to the left of me was a good friend. At one point, she invited me to one of her son's Boy Scout meetings to demonstrate to the boys how I communicated. I brought along some of my communication devices to show them. We also did some sign language. As you can tell from the picture on the next page, I think they enjoyed it.

My show-and-tell at the Boy Scout meeting.

After my job ended at AT&T, I moved to North Carolina to live near my sister Elizabeth and to attend a community college. I took a two-year program in medical records. This was a commuter college and the student population was much older than in previous schools I attended. Most were people returning to school after being laid off from long-time career jobs or they were choosing a new career path. The students had a more serious attitude toward the class work. Benefitting from that level of commitment, I graduated with honors in two years.

I returned to Kentucky and was successful in finding a job in medical records in my hometown of Louisa at the same nursing home I had worked at twenty years earlier. Coming full circle, I felt as though I had fulfilled goals that I had set years ago.

Thankfully, I was able to fulfill my goals from that strange and fateful fall semester of 1980 at Eastern Kentucky University, so long ago.

*　　*　　*　　*

One of my dream jobs as a young person was to do stand-up comedy. After I lost my speech, I forgot about being a comic, because I thought no one would laugh at a joke told on a device with an automated voice.

In 1988 I attended a conference for nonverbal persons. I was in a room full of people with various disabilities and communication methods. I moved about the room listening and looking at all the chatting.

I became engaged in a conversation with a man who used a head pointer and a letter board to spell out words. It took a long time to converse with him. He spelled a series of words while I mentally read them, not realizing at first that he was telling me a joke. By the time he finished I was laughing uproariously, complete with my characteristic snort noises. He did the same. I looked around and noticed the entire room was deep in conversation in their own way, but I could hear the CP snort from every direction. I learned that day if you're funny, it will come out. Nothing can hold that back and nothing is impossible.

*   *   *   *

Another thing I did during the eighties was attend two Women's Marches in Washington, DC, although I forget the exact years.

That's me in the shades at a Women's March in DC in the 80s

*　　*　　*　　*

Please note: The next section contains sensitive material related to suicide. If the reader feels overwhelmed, please reach out to someone you trust or to a crisis line (dial 988) for support.

In going over old writings and gathering information for this book I found something that I wrote in 1988. It was a suicide note that I now can't remember writing. I must have been in a crisis because the note is written with what looks like crayon and in almost child-like penmanship. It surprised me, because in my recollection, 1988 was a time when I thought life was going well. As I read it now, I see that having a great job at AT&T, which I had worked hard to achieve after my speech loss, did not soothe the loneliness and isolation that my stroke had created.

It wasn't the first time that I had contemplated killing myself. There were many years when dying was a daily thought. In my mind though, I would die in some accident, or be taken hostage and murdered. I wanted my life to end, but I really didn't want to do it. I thought that if someone else did it or if I were in an accident, it would be easier for my family to accept.

There have been a couple of serious narrow escapes when I could have committed the act, like that time in Van Lear, Kentucky. I knew the medications that I took daily for seizures could be used to overdose and send me into a peaceful sleep.

My secret dread from high school would come back to dwell in my brain and send me those old messages: "you're not good enough;" "you're not smart enough;" "no one will ever want you." I was terrified that I'd never be independent or capable of holding a job.

In that suicide note from 1988, I designated my belongings to charities or family members and mused about the uselessness of my dentist appointment the next day, because I wouldn't be alive to go. I talked about the endless lonely nights and the difficulty making real friends. I said, "maybe all I need is a big hug from someone who really cares. It hurts to be with people and it hurts to be alone. I have nothing to offer this world and I wish I could have made some sense of my being here."

When I look at this raw expression of frustration and helplessness, I'm thinking that putting it on paper probably saved my life. I am still looking to make sense of my being, but I've found value in my existence through prayer, writing, and a healthy appreciation of life itself.

My rock and roll pal, Elaine, and I at a concert in the 1980s when I was living in Cincinnati.

It makes you

(Written while coming out of the fog from the stroke.)

It comes out of nowhere and hits you flat between your eyes.
It shakes you up.
It makes you to want to look for answers.
It makes you scared to be the independent person you always thought you were.
It makes you think of things you've done in the past.
It makes you question your every decision and action that has brought you to this point.
It makes you wonder if you will be around to question the decisions you make today.
It makes you long for times gone by.
It makes you think of old friends.
It makes you ask why you haven't made new friends.

It makes you question the God in whom you have put all your faith.
It makes you angry, hurt, and feeling defeated.
It makes you pray.
It makes you stronger.
It gives you power.
It makes you appreciate the blessings you have TODAY.
It brings you to realize if this is the end, you are going to be okay.
It brings you closer to God in the end.

What has shaken your faith? Whatever it is, it can make you rethink your human mortality, your dependence on each other, and your need for God. It is an opportunity to appreciate every moment that you are healthy.

It Makes You

Chapter 7

Pathway to Love

Traveling the pathway to love has generated my share of disappointments and heartbreaks. Insecurity and poor self-image kept me painfully shy with the opposite sex throughout my childhood and adolescence, making it difficult for me to learn to interact socially. My early life had been a series of challenges that I handled pretty well, until high school. It was then that I felt out of place among my peers. I did not date or participate in many activities and my confidence in that arena was never developed.

My first memory of attending a formal social event was my eighth-grade dance. I don't recall wanting to go, but my mother probably encouraged me. When I arrived, people had already coupled up, and I was left sitting with a few other shy misfits in the back. As the dancing started, I remember wishing I could go home.

Then, Johnny Moore, one of the high school's volunteer chaperones, came over and asked me to dance. The song was Bridge Over Troubled Waters (a popular song of the late sixties by Simon and Garfunkel), a tune I had listened to many times from my 45-rpm record collection. Johnny was someone I knew from seeing him at school and I had good feelings about because of his easygoing, friendly nature. Once, while exiting the school bus in high school, I was carrying a load of schoolbooks and almost fell. My books went flying and landed in a pile in front of me. Before I could begin to pick them up, Johnny ran up and gathered them for me. Therefore, I was thrilled that my first slow dance was going to be with this nice person. It was an unusually long song, but I felt comfortable with his guidance on the dance floor. I will forever be grateful to Johnny, who would become a nuclear scientist at NASA, for this beautiful first dance memory. Later I would attend my junior and senior proms, but I went alone and didn't enjoy them, so no positive, lasting memories were made in that department.

My dating experiences came when I was in college. Not having any of those opportunities in high school made me very vulnerable later when I did receive attention from men. In my late teens, my self-image was still fragile, and I was eager to have a relationship with someone. This proved to be dangerous, leading to some unwise choices. I tried to grab at every prospect without regard to how it would make me feel later. I was like a hungry, stray pup gobbling up any kind of attention. Even with that reckless attitude, few occasions would come my way until my twenties. Desperation to find that someone would eventually lead to a few dead ends in the hopes of finding love.

No one likes to believe that they'd allow another person to take advantage of them, but looking back now, I can see how susceptible I was to men who could see my desperation and use it to their advantage. Too many times, I overlooked the frequent intoxication or the wandering eye just to have that brief feeling of being in love. But it was clearly not love, as I know love now.

Losing my speech at 24 created barriers that were too difficult for the average man to understand or attempt to cross. Communication on a casual basis became nearly impossible. The feelings that I would never find someone to share my life grew more intense. The men who did attempt to get to know me did so out of inquisitiveness. I did cultivate some lifelong friendships from these men who just found my oddities fascinating. At each location where I have lived, I had a close male friend, but no true romances.

After a succession of bad relationships, I decided at age 38 that I would live out my life as a single person and be grateful for my friends. I concluded that my life was full and I should not ask for more. I told my mother that I felt at peace with my single status and that I wanted to throw a big party on my 40th birthday in lieu of a wedding. How was I to know that love was just around the corner?

In 1994, I returned to my home in Louisa after earning the associate's degree in North Carolina to take the job at the senior center. Wanting to be active in my community, I joined the local Democratic Women's Club. As part of the club's fundraising efforts, they sponsored an annual bike tour called The Appalachian Bike Tour. The money raised would go to a college scholarship given each year to a deserving student in the local high school. That first year I came back, I worked the registration table for the cyclists to sign up for the ride. I registered all the cyclists. When they all returned to my table to sign in, I knew everyone returned safely. That was the first time I noticed that one cyclist. He was looking at me a lot. He asked another cyclist if he knew my name. The other cyclist, a friend from school, introduced us. His name was Mark Jackson. He had noticed people were communicating with me in Sign language and it sparked his interest because he knew a little Sign language himself.

Although he seemed to show a lot of interest in meeting me, I was resolved and happy in my independent, single life. Later that year, I began attending church with my sister and noticed a long-haired, bushy-bearded guy in the choir. I didn't recognize it was the same Mark Jackson because his bike helmet had always covered his long hair. I turned to my sister and said, "Who's the hippie in the choir?" In my teens, I had considered myself to be a flower child or a peacenik so I was intrigued by him. After church, we spoke briefly. I joined a Bible study group held at his home to get to know him better. Eventually we began to see each other regularly. Many elderly people at church approached me individually saying, "Mark is a good man. You be good to him."

The hippie in the choir

I remember one of our early evenings together when he came to my apartment to help me hand out candy on Halloween. I was still relatively new to the area and didn't know many people. I was amazed at the number of trick-or-treating children and their reactions to seeing Mark. He seemed to know every one of them. The kids and parents would greet Mark as if he was a member of their family. It warmed my heart to see children run up and be so joyful around him.

Biking was one of his hobbies. While we were dating, I asked Mark to help me find an adult-size, three-wheeled bike. It took two years, but he found a nearly junked one for twenty bucks. He refurbished it and added a steering wheel from a riding lawn mower so I could steer it one-handed. He added a hand brake, an easy-on seat, and toe clips on the pedals. We have now been riding bikes for 27 years.

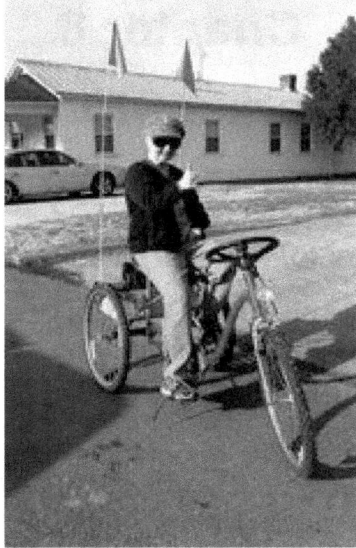

Me on the bike Mark customized for me.

At about the same time that I had my stroke in the early 1980s and lost my speech, Mark was in the next state, West Virginia, facing his own challenges. He was working hard to regain the ability to walk and talk again after a six-week coma due to a motorcycle wreck at age 16. He was left with significant physical limitations. We both worked hard to adapt to our new disabilities and we both moved to different parts of the country in attempts to start new lives. It took us coming home to find someone who would understand each other's challenges and our battles for independence.

Over the years, Mark has been a tremendous help in making alterations to make life easier for me, as I have for him.

To learn more about Mark and his life before we came together as one, keep reading!

Chapter 8

Mark's Story:

Doing What Country Boys Do

(as told by Mark Jackson)

I was born on a Marine base in North Carolina in 1963. My father was a Marine and was serving overseas when I was born. I think he was in Spain. He was from East Lynn, West Virginia, 30 miles south of Huntington. If you blinked while you were driving through it, you might miss it. My mother was from a suburb of Huntington. They had been introduced by my father's brother-in-law, my Aunt's husband, who knew them both. I was their first child. I was followed 16 months later by my sister and 12 years later by my brother. I also have three step-mothers and a number of step-siblings, but I will get into that later.

Dad got out of the Marines in 1966 and moved us back to East Lynn. We rented a house from my Papaw. The house didn't have a bathroom until my Father, Uncle and Papaw put in one. Dad went to Marshall College (now University) in Huntington and worked as a substitute teacher at a number of area schools. I remember him taking me to school with him once, I was probably three or four. I don't know if it was show-and-tell that day or what. He also worked part-time at a clothing manufacturer. Eventually, we moved into a trailer that Dad put on his parents' property. We lived about an eighth of a mile down the creek from my Papaw. Papaw and Memaw had built a new home across a 'holler' from his mother, my great-grandmother.

My Papaw was a story by himself and a great inspiration to me. He was a coal miner. Back around 1940, a mountain fell on him. It crushed his right leg and broke his back. After an extended hospital stay, he spent two years in a full body cast then the next two years tending garden from his knees.

In 1968, when I was still four, we moved to Williamstown, West Virginia, directly across the Ohio River from Marietta, Ohio, which I still think today is a beautiful town. My Dad was an industrial engineer and went to work at the Remmington Rand, Inc. plant as a timekeeper. He moved our trailer to a small trailer court in Williamstown. He didn't like that one and within a couple of weeks moved it to a larger one. After a couple of years, he was fed up with the trailer court rules. We moved downtown and rented a couple of homes in succession. One was pretty close to the river and I loved it. To this day, I still miss living close to a river.

I learned to fish when I was very young. We went camping, too, when I was a kid. I remember camping trips to Canada. On the first one, when I was still four, I caught a two-foot Northern Pike, bigger than anything my Dad caught on that trip. We did a lot of camping when I was growing up.

On one of those camping trips we went to the Ashton campground halfway between Point Pleasant and Huntington, West Virginia, where we encountered a 10-year-old boy and his dad who told us they had made a deal that when the boy turned 10, the dad would buy him a mini-bike. I said to my dad "that sounds good; why can't we make the same deal?" So we did. That's how I ended up with my first motor bike. We also met and became good friends with my next year's 1st grade teacher. My mom told her of the "deal" because she mentioned it once in class when I had her again as my 3rd grade teacher.

About this same time, when I was in the fourth grade, I was on a Pop Warner football team. I would go to all the practices during the week, but we were camping almost every weekend and I never made it to the games. I ended up playing a few minutes at the end of the last game of the season. At 60 pounds, I was kind of small for a defensive end. I got ran over on my first play, but made a tackle for a loss on my second.

Me on my motorbike around the age of 10.

I ended up playing football into my sophomore year in high school. I quit two weeks before the end of the season. I wasn't getting to play any of the varsity games and not very many of the junior varsity games. The roster listed me at 115 pounds and I was still on the line. I skipped practice one day. When I got home I found my dad on the roof of our 2-story house extremely tired from laying blocks. I climbed the scaffolding to the roof and laid the last 22-pound block, I said to myself," that's it, I'm needed at home."

Me just shy of my 13th birthday.

On December 27th, 1973, we moved to a 40-acre farm between Cambridge and New Concord, Ohio. We had about 20 head of cattle, chickens, Guinea hens, a couple of turkeys, a couple of ponies, rabbits, pigs, dogs, a cat, and some of Memaw's geese we brought with us from East Lynn. We really didn't need the dogs because the geese took care of anything that was bothering the Guineas.

I loved it on the farm. My grades even improved. I went from just getting by in the fourth grade to straight Bs. In December of the next year, however, Memaw was killed in an automobile accident and we were moving again. We went back to East Lynn in early 1975. Dad had to help Papaw.

Dad had to quit his job at that plant at that point and he scrambled to make ends meet in East Lynn. I was not yet 12, but I was helping him cut mine timbers and bale hay and do other odd jobs. I was just doing what country boys do. Soon he got a job at a men's clothing store, but he kept doing the odd jobs and I kept helping him.

Me, on the right, and my family, 1977 or '78

My mother was mostly a stay-at-home Mom although she did work at a day care center when we were living in Williamstown. When I was 14, she was diagnosed with liver cancer. After a 14-month struggle, she died in October of 1978. Having three motherless kids might have influenced my father's decision to remarry in March of 1979.

I always did pretty well in school. I was on the honor roll from the sixth grade through the tenth grade. Three days before the end of my sophomore year, at the age of 16, I had a motorcycle accident. It permanently changed my life and any plans I might have had at the time.

My Dad had been a motorcycle racer and had performed in motorcycle rodeos. As I mentioned earlier, I was riding at the age of 10. I learned to ride rounding up cattle on our farm in Ohio, doing what country boys do.

I do not remember the accident at all. I think the kick stand came down unexpectedly hitting the dirt road on our farm that I was traveling on, throwing the motorcycle to the ground. It sent me tumbling 40 feet through the woods. I ended up banging my head on a white oak tree. The base of my helmet struck the tree, right where my injury occurred. I was 200 feet from my house. My step-brother saw it happen and told my father.

I spent the next six weeks in a coma. As the saying goes, it was a miracle I survived. The doctors at the Cabel Hospital in Huntington actually told my family to prepare for the worse. They didn't think I could make it. Oddly, when I was in the coma, I was aware of people in the room with me and I could hear them talk, but I couldn't respond.

I surprised everybody when I woke up from the coma. Shortly after that, I was sent home. I had a traumatic brain injury. My speech was slurred and my mobility was severely impaired. I did receive a visit weekly from a therapist, but otherwise I was pretty much left to rehab on my own.

My stepmother tried to do some physical therapy like they showed her at the hospital. All I remember is she was hurting me and I was fighting back. Although I was out of the coma, I really don't think I was fully conscious for some time. I just felt someone pulling on my arms and legs, and I got mean and I fought. It was just a big mess and home was the last place on earth that I wanted to be. She seemed to go out of her way to make things rougher on me. She didn't want a "cripple" in the house. I think she ended up blaming me for her eventual divorce from my father. Before she died, she sent word through my aunt that she forgave me, but I didn't think I had anything to be forgiven for.

I would walk around the farm and gradually build up my strength. To help my thinking processes, I once took a back tire off a bike that wasn't working and tore the bike down into parts. Through trial and error, I was eventually able to re-assemble it.

My uncle lived nearby and my sister and cousin got me on a bicycle very soon after I came home. First, I could ride 10 yards and then 100. I grew to love biking. At one point, 20 years ago, I could bike 60 miles in one day.

Before my accident, my plan was to join the Army after high school and get training to become a truck driver. I saw myself being an over-the-road semi driver. My father wanted me to go to a trade school. Neither of those options were possible now. In March of 1981, I went to the West Virginia Rehabilitation Center, operated by the West Virginia Department of Vocational Rehabilitation, to be evaluated for future training and employment possibilities. While there, I met a deaf girl who taught me the ASL alphabet and a few signs. This would prove very useful later in life when I would need to interpret for Tina. I was sent home after four months to return to high school and graduate with my class on time with the people that I had been in school with since the 6th grade.

I stayed with my aunt and her family the first 6 weeks of my senior year. She could see what was going on at my home. She was a social worker with the Department of Human Services. She saw similar situations every day. By this time, Dad was a coal miner and my aunt could see me being thrown from pillar to post by people who were in the mindset of keeping me hidden from the public, That's just what backwoods folks did. Many didn't take time to ask what was available for a child.

Here is an example. When I was 16 and just out of the coma, Sunday morning would roll around and we would go to church, Dad would carry me, all 5'7", 89 pounds of me, in and set me on the church pew. After church one Sunday, Bernard Ross and Joe Trautwine got to me before Dad did. Bernard had been one of my volunteer assistant football coaches. Bernard said, "Let's try something new, put your hand on my shoulder, and me and Joe won't let you fall," and I walked out of church that day. Dad never carried me again. That must have been late August or September 1980, because I remember camping on Labor Day weekend at East Lynn Lake

and my Papaw convincing me that my right arm wasn't paralyzed and that I could rest it on the arm of the wheelchair.

After graduation I went back to the West Virginia rehab center for evaluation. I was happy to go back. My father couldn't understand it, but the situation at home with my stepmother was intolerable. My dad told me to try to get into plumbing because there would always be a need for plumbers. They evaluated me on putting galvanized pipe together and I did well, but they didn't offer plumbing training. Also, I might have partied too much and caused the evaluators to give up on me. I wanted to go into small engine repair. They gave me a diagram of a big engine (a V-8) and told me to trace the route of a spark. I guess I flunked because I was going home again. Also, I might have been a little too smart aleck for them. One time when they asked what I wanted to do for a job, I said I wanted to be a hitman for the mob. I don't think they cared for that answer. On the way back home, my Dad said "well, you can clean up the workshop for your therapy and we'll get you signed up for SSI."

When I got on SSI, I was due some back pay. My Dad used it to buy my sister, Sherrie, a junk-pile-of-a-car that she could supposedly use to run me places. By this time, he was a coal miner and could have bought her a new one, or at least a good used car. Oh well, after 40 years, I see things differently. Then after another fight with my Dad, I promised him that as soon as there was an opening at a local apartment building, I would move out. I was angry after the accident and fought a lot. I had enough of fighting. I remember at least one black eye. I would get angry before the accident, too, but didn't fight because I didn't want to get in trouble.

My stepmother and one of her sons would sit on the sofa and watch my sister and me wash dishes. Things like that would get me angry. It still doesn't take much to get me riled. I made good on my promise though. I lived in my own apartment for a year and a half.

Dad had begun divorce proceedings before I moved out, believe it or not. He would come home and tell me his lawyer mentioned having me arrested for fighting so much. The lawyer is an elected official now, but if I still lived in West Virginia, I wouldn't vote for him for dogcatcher. In May of 1983, my sister, who still lived in East Lynn, picked me up to attend her graduation ceremony. I knew my Dad was dating another woman seriously and I asked my sister if Dad and Linda were going to get married? She laughed and said, "They already are married. They ran off to somewhere and did it."

The coal mine where Dad worked shut down and he turned to the family trade, carpentry. My Papaw was a carpenter as were his three sons. They all learned the trade and all three joined the military. Dad started doing carpentry work, but in a depressed area of West Virginia he was barely breaking even, so he decided to move to Florida. Two days before the family was to leave, I decided to go with them to take care of my little brother, Darran. I couldn't imagine someone in childcare hurting him. So in 1984 I moved to Florida with two trash bags of clothes and my three-wheeled bike tied to the space between the truck and the trailer.

We moved to Tequesta, Florida, near Jupiter and about 15 miles north of West Palm Beach. I rode my trike to the beach a lot, so often it got boring, so I went to the local bicycle shop and became an intern bike mechanic. That was one of the high points of being in Florida. I worked at the bike shop for a year. It was operated by Dominic ànd Ralph, two Christian brothers who will always be remembered and loved by me. Ralph was legally blind, yet he taught me to "true" wheels, which opened up a whole different world of understanding to me. Dominic taught me so much about bikes and the Church. The bike shop was a phenomenal life experience for me. I met some of the most interesting, nicest everyday people. One day, I missed meeting Burt Reynolds and Lonnie Anderson by about ten minutes. I had left for the day to be home when my brother got out of school. They came in to rent bikes.

I did meet the late, great Tammy Wynette when her daughter, Georgette Jones, was baptized at my Church. Georgette and I remain good friends through Facebook to this day. I have not seen her since 1994 when I went with my then-girlfriend to the York (Pennsylvania) Creation Festival, a contemporary Christian music festival. I got to sit backstage with DC Talk, a Christian rap and rock trio, Geoff Moore, a Christian singer, and others. After the festival, my girlfriend drove me home to Ft. Gay, West Virginia, I fell asleep on the couch, she got up a little mad at me for not waking her, and she headed back to Nashville. My wife, Tina, now likes to say she's the one that got away. By the way, she and her now husband were coincidentally married on Tina's birthday

*   *   *   *

I did have some adventures in Florida. In 1985 or maybe early 1986 my Dad, my future brother-in-law and I went fishing off the coast of Juno Beach, 10 miles south of the Jupiter Inlet. We were 4 miles off the coast. Dad was reeling in fish like crazy and he was so hateful with me, I just reeled my line in and put my pole in the holder and observed. I noticed we were taking on water. I told Dad and he responded with "I'm having too much fun catchin' fish."

There's a working lighthouse at the Jupiter Inlet and we never lost sight of the lighthouse all day. We had come out about 2:00 PM. About 4:30 Dad realized water is ankle deep in the boat where he was standing so he reeled in his line and immediately started the engine. The engine was so small for that size boat it had to be full throttled. We had three flares, and two of them had gotten wet and were no good. The one that was good went off and danced around my feet before burning out in the floor of the boat.

What are we going to do now? Dad was able to detach the boat mirror and, with the last of the sun's rays, signal another boat who had a radio who reported our peril to the Coast Guard. By this time, we had been in the Gulfstream and drifted a few hundred feet north of the Inlet under the bright light of the lighthouse. With my glasses I had 20/25 vision and it being dark now, I looked over towards the coast and there it was, the blue flashing light of the Coast Guard looking for us. I told Dad to have the radio guy tell them where we were. The Coast Guard came and pulled us clean to the Port of Palm Beach where my future brother-in law called my stepmother to come get him so he could retrieve his jeep that had the boat trailer.

Upon arrival of the boat trailer they backed it down as far as possible Dad hooked the cable to the loose eye on the boat. They winched it about halfway on the trailer and pulled it out of the water, actually bending the trailer up in front of the wheel. Dad pulled the drain plug and for 45 minutes a solid stream of water drained from between the hull and deck. This answered the question of why it was so low in the water when full throttled; all that water immediately ran to the back of the boat and, along with the weight of the motor, in addition to a wave breaking over the engine, shorted out everything, which began the dilemma. Dad told me when I later came home from college in Chicago that he found a little hole in the hull right below my seat. It looked like the end of a screw or bolt had punctured the fiberglass hull.

*   *   *   *

I had a girlfriend when I lived in Florida. She helped me quite a bit. In 1987, she moved to Columbia, South Carolina. When she left, I went to Chicago, Illinois, to attend the Moody Bible Institute.

I was at Moody for three semesters and for three summer school terms. The Institute is a fully accredited Christian college with campuses now in Chicago and Spokane, Washington, and seminaries in Chicago and Plymouth, Michigan. The Chicago campus was north of the downtown loop at the corner of Chicago Avenue and North LaSalle Drive. I remember stepping outside of the college on North LaSalle Drive and saying to myself, "If my friends could see me now," then I would ask myself, "What am I doing here?"

I loved PCM (Practical Christian Ministry). I, along with three or four classmates, accompanied a man named Lou Sorry, and we would pass out tracts and witness for the Lord down on Michigan Avenue or Division Street. Lou would do his "ladder art" and explain the gospel about how Jesus Christ bridged the gap between mankind and His Father and we just had to ask him to forgive us and give him control of our lives.

One of my buddies was always with me, to keep me from getting in a fight, I guess. I loved street preaching and visiting the Illinois State Hospital. When it was cold, we would take our preaching to the subway.

After summer school in 1989, I went to Allegon, Michigan, to serve as a camp counselor for six weeks. I did it the next summer, too. It was a Christian camp. The first week of the second year was a retreat for Army troops who had married Korean brides. We counselors washed dishes for them. When one wife bowed to me, it was very humbling. The second week was day camp for local Kalamazoo kids, then the next four weeks were for Chicago kids.

I knew I wasn't going back to school when camp was over the second summer because my grades weren't good enough. I called my Dad for advice about what to do and he said I should head back to West Virginia. I had all of my stuff from college, seven or eight boxes full, shipped to my Granny in Columbus Ohio. I stayed with her and her husband, Dale, for about a month. That's how long it took for me to get on their nerves. I think I was a bit too smart aleck for my Granny. Also, she wanted me to shave and I wouldn't do it. I took the Greyhound to Huntington, West Virginia. I then moved into an apartment in Ft. Gay, West Virginia, a small river town at the juncture of the Tug and Big Sandy Rivers. It was adjacent to Louisa, Kentucky. I moved in on September 4th, 1989. My "Great Northern Adventure" was over. I was never ordained, but I am always ready to tell of the hope that I have in the Lord.

I was still living there when I first met Tina. I remember it as 1994, not 1995. I was participating in the bicycle tour when she was volunteering. Shortly thereafter Tina sent word through her sister asking me if I knew of any three-wheeled bikes in the area. I didn't, but I said I would keep my eye out for one. Two years later I found one to give to her, then I modified or customized it to her needs. And that was where it all began.

Tina and I riding in a fundraising event for St. Jude's hospital. I rode 11 miles that day.

Chapter 9:

Marriage
(back to Tina)

July 25, 1998 – Our wedding day

Our journeys had come together. Even though I was seven years older and we didn't meet until our thirties, our similar life experiences made us feel as though we had known each other all our lives - from our very first meeting. There was only one thing we could do.

My sisters planned our wedding. We married on July 25th, 1998. Close family members cooked all the food. My cousin and aunt did the music. Friends from college drove long distances to be with me. I looked around and saw so much love coming my way. My husband's family was just as involved. So much love that day for Mark and me. Our love is still going strong almost 30 years later.

We've encouraged each other to grow and learn to be better people, inspired each other to strive further in life, and supported each other to do things we couldn't do alone. I helped him learn to drive and earn his driver's license; he has helped me attain and enjoy the opportunities of biking, owning a house, and having a dog. He applauds my efforts in writing and art. But the most important gift he has given me is prolonged independence.

*   *   *   *

In one way, our decision to marry had some fearful implications.

Boy meets girl. They fall in love, get married and live happily ever after. That is how it should be in a democracy. But if one or both of the lovebirds are disabled or elderly and receive Supplemental Security Income (SSI), not so fast. This legal union can often result in the loss of life-sustaining benefits for one or both of the lovebirds, including food stamps, rent assistance and healthcare, because of the federal "marriage penalties."

SSI is a needs-based federal program that helps people with disabilities (as well as people who are elderly) who have little or no income. It provides cash to meet basic needs for food, clothing, and shelter. If two people receiving SSI get married, they will receive 25% less in benefits than they did as two individuals. The theory is that a couple can live on less income together than they can as individuals. In addition, even if a couple doesn't get legally married, they can be considered to be "holding out" as if they are presenting themselves as a couple by SSI definition. For them, the same rules apply as for a married couple and they will have their benefits reduced. If only one person in the couple is receiving SSI, the benefit will still be reduced or they may no longer be eligible for it at all. There is also a resource limit; the amount of money you can have in the bank for an individual by SSI rules is $2,000, but for a couple it is only $3,000.

Beyond these marriage-related SSI benefit and asset restrictions, eligibility for SSI in most states means eligibility for Medicaid. Medicaid covers services not covered by other health insurance plans such as a personal care aids, "certain" durable medical equipment, medications, and transportation to medical appointments. So anything affecting SSI eligibility may have a ripple effect.

Obviously, loss of SSI or Medicaid benefits can be devastating, life-changing and even life-threatening to a person with disabilities. And that is why there is a national movement to get this changed. Marriage penalties are affecting real people in America.

As Mark and I stood up in our church in front of our family and friends in 1998 and said our vows to each other, we were unaware of the problems we would soon face with Mark's benefits. We just knew all the challenges we had overcome to get to this day. We did know our joined lives would be filled with new challenges. but we were not ready to be further punished by our own government.

The stroke I suffered at 24 years left me with vision loss and loss of my speech. Even though I was born with Cerebral palsy and suffered the stroke, I was able to work for many years. At age 40, I would go on Social Security Disability Insurance (SSDI). When I met my future husband, Mark was unable to do traditional employment because of the brain injury he had acquired when he was 16. As a result, unlike me, he did not have a work record to qualify him for Social Security Disability Insurance so he was getting SSI, medical care, and food stamps and lived in low-income housing. He managed to overcome many of the effects of his injury and live an independent life.

Within two years of knowing each other, we decided to marry. We were both stubbornly independent. Even our pastor jokingly referred to the work it would take for us to compromise on issues.

At the time, we were ignorant of how getting married would affect Mark's benefits. I was still working so my income made him ineligible for any benefits. Mark was an avid cyclist, but he quit riding for fear that he could get injured and have high medical costs.

We chose to marry out of love and our religious beliefs. It is a decision we almost regretted. We had to come up with a plan to obtain at least medical coverage for Mark. My body could not sustain a full-time job by age 40 and I easily qualified for disability, Medicaid and Medicare. We developed a plan for Mark to have a small business doing lawn care so he could file taxes on his earnings to earn enough points (20) to qualify him for disability and medical coverage. It took 17 years of paying into Social Security for him to finally qualify. Those years were back breaking for Mark and we never believed t was fair to penalize Mark because I had an income.

Many disabled Americans have to choose between a loving marriage or life-saving benefits. We as disabled people have the right to marry. The over 65 population faces the same penalties. Many choose not to legalize their union, but even living together can be considered being married.

Mark and I now both receive disability and medical coverage. It is a great comfort for Mark to have medical coverage because he has needed serious medical attention since qualifying. We are in no ways financially stable and we struggle month to month. Mark has paid a high price for trying to work. He suffers knee pain and had many cuts and bruises in falls due to his poor balance. But we have survived many obstacles in our 27 years of marriage. It was because of our stubborn determination to meet all the qualifications we have been able to live a fairly comfortable life.

Chapter 10:
Assistive Technology

In 1998, the year I married Mark, while still at the medical records job, I began to have more difficulty eating and drinking. Swallowing tests showed I was aspirating. In addition, the stress of my job, which often meant fifty-hour weeks, was causing increased anxiety. All of this led to malnutrition and dehydration which eventually required me to have a PEG (percutaneous endoscopic gastrostomy) feeding tube. After three attempts at career jobs, each one taking a larger toll on my body and health, I decided that I couldn't risk it anymore and left the traditional work force.

Becoming dependent on a feeding tube tugged at the last thread of my sanity. Another problem arose when I couldn't operate my feeding process with only one hand. Mark was eager to think of a solution, which led to the creation of Mark's patent-pending, feeding-tube stand, thought to be the first of its kind, the Jackson Peg Tube Stand. It was portable, adjustable, and operable with one hand, so users could eat without assistance. This was an answer to the cumbersome liquid food hanging from an IV pole or an unwieldy pump, both difficult for one person to handle. Fast forward: the device is now patented and has been sold all over the world. See what love can do?

I was now self-employed, at home, doing marketing and selling the Jackson Peg Tube Stand. The device has helped many people regain or maintain their independence, by acting as an extra hand to manage bolus tube fed meals with little or no assistance. It allows me to enjoy meals in any location, including at restaurants and business functions. We've sold stands to people throughout the United States and England and have had inquiries from New Zealand and

Canada. Email has become my most common method of business communication.

*   *   *   *

Living in a time of great advancements in technology of all kinds has always been counted among my many blessings. As a person born with disabilities in the 1950s with mild cerebral palsy, the availability and choice of assistive technology was extremely limited.

When I was two, I went to special classes to learn how to dress with one hand. We'd practice these tasks on a teddy bear dressed in zip-up pants, a button-up shirt, and lace-up shoes. This class was where I first encountered a person with a disability who was employed, my teacher who used a wheelchair. For me, I'd be able to complete my education through college, earning my Bachelor of Science degree in social work, with nothing more than a leg brace.

After I lost my speech and part of my vision, I had to reassess my abilities for employment. But the first thing I needed was a way to communicate. The search for a suitable communication device for an active, ambulatory woman in the early 80s proved to be very frustrating. Not only were they big and heavy and made to be mounted on wheelchairs, but they all had a man's voice!

My first device was called a Handy Voice. It was overly complicated, with a number pad that required typing in a three-digit code for each phonic sound. A single word required typing in three or four, three-digit codes. You'd really need to be a person with a strong desire to communicate to make the effort to memorize all the codes, but that was me. I became quite facile with it, though it was still slow and cumbersome in a work setting.

In 1985, after completing office training at the Perkins Center and securing the job as a clerk at AT&T, communication had to be fast and clear. I was introduced to the TTY, a device used by the deaf to make telephone calls through a relay service. It was light, with a keyboard and screen to display my words. It proved to be a highly effective method of communication for work and for phone calls.

Ten years later, I would benefit again from advances in technology. I was able to use a communication device with a woman's voice and a keyboard like the TTY. It had memory in the form of small cassette tapes. Unfortunately, its size was still an issue; it was unwieldy to carry. I used this device in conjunction with the TTY on my next job in medical records. I also had access to a powerchair on that job, provided by my employer.

I got help again from Vocational Rehabilitation services to acquire my last two communication devices, each one smaller with a better-quality female voice. My current device has allowed me to be a presenter at several events, including as keynote speaker at the Perkin's Center graduation in 2011 (see Appendix B) .

I've become dependent on a powerchair for long distances and travel. It allows me to attend conferences and big crowd events with no risks of falling and boosts my confidence to be more active.

My "independence" now depends on my computer, my communication device, my iPad, my powerchair, my walking cart, my text reader, my peg tube stand and a whole bunch of power chargers.

*   *   *   *

Sometimes, I have used my muteness in humorous ways. I have often pretended to be deaf if I was in the company of someone I found boring or unpleasant, usually with guys trying to pick me up. It would work and I was left alone. However, there was one occurrence when it did not go as planned.

I was home alone, not expecting company. It was some time in the nineties when Mark was out a lot mowing his lawns.

This particular day the doorbell rang. Being alone, I was apprehensive about opening the door. I peeked out and saw two ladies with booklets in their hands and dressed conservatively. I immediately knew they were Jehovah's Witnesses. I was bored and feeling a little mischievous, so I decided to open the door.

They were very nice and gave me their material. They began explaining the reason for their visit. I knew I was not going to be won over to their beliefs so I smiled and pointed to my ear as if to say I can't hear. The nice ladies immediately understood and we parted ways smiling and waving goodbye.

The next weekend I was again home alone when the doorbell rang. When I peeked out, I saw the two nice ladies and another younger person. I thought well they misunderstood my gestures about being deaf. They were certainly persistent, I thought. I opened the door to lots of smiles and gestures. Then the younger girl started to sign to me. I realized they had found someone to communicate with me. This won my heart so I opened the door and chatted. I found out that the girl was an intern at the university where I had graduated. We talked about the school and very little about the church, but they were able to connect with me and I appreciated the effort they made. After that, I would see the ladies again from time to time in town. We always say hello.

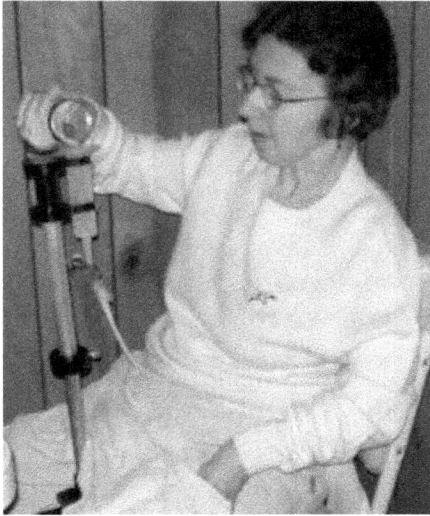

Me using the Jackson Peg Stand

Got dem old bathroom door blues

When I gotta go and the door weighs a ton
got smashed up fingers and broke up toes
Gettin it open just ain't no fun
a few of my bathroom door woes

I got one good hand and one good leg
Another trip and another bruise
Please open, I plead, as I push and beg
I got them old bathroom door blues

I try to open the door with my wheelchair
I gotta go but the door won't budge
my wheels spin and this ain't fair
I go again with another nudge
Got them old bathroom door blues

Why is it so hard to go to the John
But them bathroom blues is everywhere
These doors were made by engineers?, come on!
But To say this out loud I do not dare
Got them old bathroom door blues

I gotta go and go I do, to the door
It's not open and then I am mad
Cause my foot and arm will be sore
Open doors would make me glad
I got them old bathroom door blues

Chapter 11:
Home Ownership

Buying a house with the help of a realtor proved challenging. In 2000, my mother and I were taking our daily walk-and-talk when we spotted a house for sale. It had a big front porch which attracted me to it. There was a garage and a workshop space that I knew Mark could use for his business. There was a little backyard and I immediately pictured it as a perfect place for a dog. Mark and I had both grown up with dogs and we wanted a small dog to add to our family.

Mom said, "you know you could buy this house." The thought never crossed my mind before she said it. For days afterward we walked by and took notes. At the time, Mark and I were renting an apartment and paying a considerable amount for rent. Mark had his lawn care business going. He was having to store his mowers in the garage at our apartment. The landlord was not happy to have oil in his garage. We also had discussed buying a home for the investment and equity. The fence needed replacing, but it was doable.

We started talking about home ownership and going over our finances. Excited about the possibility of having a house and dog and lots of workspace for Mark, we called the realtor to make an appointment to view the house. He was an older man who had been in the real estate business for many years in Louisa. I had heard he was difficult when negotiating a sale.

We were able to set up a time in the next day or two. Mark and I and my mother met him at the house. After a brief tour of the house and yard, the realtor talked to my mother as if she were the buyer. When he found out that Mark and I were the buyers, he bluntly asked, "Do you have money?" This enraged us all and my mom spoke up and said "you don't worry about the money." What he did not know was we had already been approved for the loan at a bank out of town. We were also able to make a sizable down payment.

His question was inappropriate and judgmental and I wished we didn't have to work with him. But he was the listing realtor, so we continued considering whether this was the property we wanted to buy. In the meantime, the realtor was doing some investigative work by asking local folks about us.

When we met again for another look at the house, his disposition had changed dramatically after receiving positive reports of our characters and credit. After learning the price and evaluating our finances, we talked to a bank in the next town about a mortgage. It was approved. We determined that the payments, upkeep, and taxes would be within our means.

We returned to the realtor to pay the down payment. He then tried to persuade us to get the mortgage with his bank for a higher interest rate on the premise that he didn't think our bank would appraise it for the selling price. We declined his numerous attempts to get us to switch banks. I decided to make him a document saying he would return our down payment if the appraisal did not pass. He was a little taken aback and said, "Just to show you I trust you more than you trust me I am going to give you the keys today!" All went smoothly after he signed my little agreement and we bought our first and only house. We moved into the house in 2001 and added a new fence and a rescue mutt to the backyard. Mark used the garage and workshop for his business and I got a great porch where we often sit.

*   *   *   *

The realtor's initial behavior has not been an uncommon reaction from people upon first meeting us; they see two bodies with disabilities and assume we're unable to take care of our own business. We had learned to not bring anyone with us while house hunting because the realtors would want to talk to them instead of Mark and me.

Potential employers have proven to be another group of people who are fast to form opinions. For every successful job interview I've had there were many more unsuccessful ones. I could tell the job interview was going to be a futile exercise during the first two minutes because I saw "the look." It's the look I often see on people's faces when they watch me walk into view for the first time. It is one of puzzlement and disapproval. "The look" always makes me feel hopeless, although I have learned when to expect it and how to handle it most of the time.

Often these problems with other's first impressions and the prejudice that follows have occurred with people in the medical profession. One of the first incidents that I can remember is when my beloved pediatrician, Guy Cunningham was retiring and a young physician was taking over his practice. I was fourteen years old on my first visit to him. Sitting alone in an exam room waiting, I heard the new doctor and his nurse approach the door, reach for my chart, and thumb through the pages. Then I heard him say, "She has cerebral palsy. Is she spoiled rotten?" I don't recall what the nurse said, but I remember how the words stung me and how I never wanted to come back. At fourteen years of age, it was time for me to change doctors anyway.

From repeated experiences, it seems as if doctors form instant opinions of people with a diagnosis of cerebral palsy. Once I went to a new dentist at the age of thirty-three. After reading my chart, the doctor came out to the waiting room and asked, "Is your mommy with you today?"

There were the doctors at the University of Kentucky Medical Center where I was taken after my stroke who accused my family of overreacting to my loss of speech. Their assumption was that I never spoke and didn't see this as an acute situation, even after being told of my public speaking class in college and various other pieces of evidence that I did indeed speak. They talked to my family as if they were going from doctor to doctor, searching for some miracle cure. Once they were convinced this was a new symptom, they accused me of taking drugs which brought on the stroke. After a battery of tests, they were unable to determine the cause of my cerebral vascular incident, but offered no assistance or therapy for someone they believed was not having any new problems.

My last dentist, who I thought somewhat knew me, began our first post-stroke session by gesturing wildly with his hands, mimicking brushing teeth. This was his way of inquiring as to whether or not I knew how to brush my teeth. I was in my thirties. Not only did he think I needed instructions on how to brush my teeth, but he also thought I was deaf!

There's a doctor I've seen on and off for many years. He still feels the need to yell at me every time we're in his small exam room. It doesn't matter how many times I tell him, "Hey, doc, I'm not deaf." I would think the medical profession would have become more enlightened over the years, but it continues to happen time after time.

It's not only doctors and potential employers who make judgmental first impressions. Once in a self-serve shoe store I was trying on several pairs of shoes on a bench provided by the store. I noticed another customer watching me as I laced and tied shoes with one hand until she could no longer control herself. She ran over, pulled the shoe out of my hand, shoved it on my foot and began doing the laces. I was so surprised by her jackrabbit pounce that I was unable to stop her. After she had both shoes on me, I just nodded my head and she walked away. I wound up not buying the shoes - too much lacework and of course I wouldn't have the impatient customer helping me put them on every day! As good-hearted as some people's actions are meant to be, they can still be irritating.

Once, a friend and I planned to meet for the weekend in Lexington at a hotel. I lost my way and spotted a woman at an ATM machine in a bank parking lot. I wrote a note requesting directions to the hotel and began walking toward her to deliver it. When she noticed me walking her way she stood up and started waving me off, saying, "No, no! Go away! Just go away!" I guess the sight of a limping woman with a note made her think I was panhandling for money.

I'm tired of being angry at these unfortunate situations. I'm often mistaken for being deaf and that's okay, but when people also assume I have a childlike mentality and I'm not able to understand what's being said to me, my eyes flare red and my blood pressure rises. It might be easier to defuse if I were able to speak and tell them politely that I'm disabled and I may not be able to do many, many things, but I do understand English. However, if given enough time, I can typically change their first impressions quickly.

William Shakespeare wrote, "Heat not a furnace for your foe that it do singe yourself." I feel like I burn myself when I get angry. I know I'm going to continuously encounter these discouraging situations in my life. So, as a Christian, how do I control my anger and frustration at my own limitations, and to those around me who jump to these incorrect conclusions? I've come to realize that it's a daily choice, to alter my reactions to these "insults", and to work to change the views of others just by being myself.

Our house in Louisa. Paid off! We love it.

Chapter 12:
My Advocacy Work

This may sound strange, but, through most of my life, I did not think of myself as disabled. I was the way I was and I did the things I needed to do. I certainly didn't consider myself part of a larger "disability community." I had never considered advocacy work until my second stay at the Perkins Center. Barbara Pugh, the Center Director at the time, asked me about serving on the Commonwealth Council on Developmental Disability (CCDD), a state administered, federally funded policy group. I believe this was around 2010. I had never heard of such a thing.

As I mentioned earlier in this book, I had been involved in advocating for women's rights and attended demonstrations for the ERA (Equal Rights Amendment) in DC twice in college. Before that my father influenced me as I saw him working for poor farmers by teaching them to access resources from the government. And we had that family history of union activism. I decided to give this disability advocacy thing a try. That's how I started my advocacy work.

In 2010, I was asked to speak at a training conference for staff of the Kentucky Office of Vocational Rehabilitation. This was my first overt effort at disability advocacy. I gave my speech using my augmentative communication device. You can find the text of my speech in Appendix A. The next year, I was asked to speak to the 2011 graduating class of the Perkins Rehabilitation Center. Again, I used my aug comm device and, as mentioned before, the text of that speech is in Appendix B.

Over the years, I have applied to serve on a number of Kentucky state advisory boards and councils. At various times, I have been appointed to Commonwealth Council of Developmental Disability, the Kentucky Assistive Technology

Services (KATS) Network Advisory Council, the Kentucky Protection and Advocacy Board, and the Kentuckians for the Commonwealth Board. These associations led to opportunities to advocate in many different ways and to meet many new people.

My partner and soulmate in this journey has always been Mark. He has been with me in every venture, every Council or Board meeting, every rally or protest, often interpreting for me as I signed to him what I wanted to say. I guess you could say I have radicalized him.

In 2012, I was appointed to the Commonwealth Council on Developmental Disabilities (CCDD). CCDD is Kentucky's Development Disabilities Planning Council. The Kentucky CCDD is made up of 26 citizens appointed by the Governor. Eight of the Council members are representatives of state agencies and the remaining 18 members are divided equally among individuals with developmental disabilities and representatives of individuals with developmental disabilities, usually family members. I was appointed as an individual with a disability.

In 2013, the CCDD began researching the possibility of creating an Asset-Based Community Development (ABCD) project in Kentucky. The goal of an ABCD is to enhance opportunities for inclusion of individuals with developmental disabilities. In October of 2013, the CCDD invited members from other state councils who were doing this work to come talk to the council. In January 2014, we hired consultants to help us start the initiative. We began training and named the project "Community of Sharing".

I was selected to initiate a Community of Sharing in Eastern Kentucky. To prepare for this task I attended a conference on community building in Toronto to learn about Asset Based Community Development. I took my sister Elizabeth with me.

I have to share a story about my visit to Canada. A group of us participants decided to go downtown to watch a drag show at a little bar. When we got there, we saw that the bar was not accessible. The owner saw my dilemma and told us to meet him at the back door. He and a few patrons got to work and tore apart two tables to make a workable ramp for me to get in the bar. There I was in Toronto to learn about inclusion and I just had experienced the biggest gesture to include me. The queens loved it and came to my table during breaks for song requests. As I left at the end of the evening the owner and others made sure I got out safely. He said, "Next time you come I will have a proper ramp here." I felt good about making him aware of accessibility.

On July 1, 2014, the CCDD contracted with Kentucky Self-Advocates for Freedom, a non-profit, to take on the Community of Sharing Program in Louisa and Westwood as a project. KYSAFF would also be working to take the "Community of Sharing" concept to other Kentucky communities. Self-advocates across the state were to be key to making the program successful.

The plan used the principles of Asset Based Community Development which focused on engaging with the community members to identify and celebrate individual and community talents, skills and assets involving citizens with and without disabilities, rather than focusing on problems and needs. The goal was to improve the community by actively listening to everyone, learning what the community had to offer and working toward common community goals for the betterment of all. It did not focus on just the disabled, but by making an effort to include everyone, it would be wholly inclusive. To introduce our project in Louisa and Westwood, I wrote the following article for the Exceptional Family Magazine, a twice-yearly publication of the CCDD.

Community of Sharing: CCDD Launches Plan to Promote Inclusion by Building on Community Talents and Interests

This article originally appeared in the Kentucky Exceptional Family Magazine and is used with permission from the Commonwealth Council on Developmental Disabilities.

Try to imagine that where you live is a place where everyone is valued and respected. Imagine that people are interested in you and the special gifts that you could share with the community. Imagine that your community welcomes all people regardless of their differences because not only is it right but because with every unique person there is a new gift or talent added to the community. This is the goal that the Commonwealth Council on Developmental Disabilities in Kentucky is working to accomplish. The Council is taking the first steps to initiate a community enrichment plan called "Community of Sharing." The plan will help communities in Kentucky not only be more inclusive but allow all citizens to become actively involved in what happens where they live.

The plan uses the principles of Asset Based Community Development. Rather than focusing on problems and needs, ABCD engages with community members to identify and celebrate individual and community talents, skills and assets involving citizens with and without disabilities. The goal is to improve the community through people and community-centered supports by actively listening to everyone, learning what the community has to offer and working toward common goals for the betterment of all. The effort does not focus on just the disabled but by making an effort to include everyone, it will be wholly inclusive.

The Council has chosen two areas in Eastern Kentucky to initiate this plan and selected two council members from each area to oversee the project. The two areas are Lawrence County, a rural setting, and Westwood near Ashland, a more urban setting. Tina Jackson was selected to initiate the plan in Lawrence County and David Minor in Westwood. Each area selected will develop different-looking models because the initiative encourages the input of local people.

The first step is to listen to community members and learn what they want to do to improve their community. As people express their wants and realize what the talents are within their own community, it gives them the strength and desire to work together. This work strengthens relationships and creates a strong will to realize the common goal. Community-centered resources give citizens a real investment in the work.

The effort in Lawrence County and Westwood is just beginning, but it has become obvious that people are eager to embrace the process and start the work. Five part-time "community builders" have been hired to start the development of community plans. Several wants already have been uncovered. In Westwood, there is a communal interest in classic cars and the rebuilding of old cars. This could be developed into the creation of a classic car club that would allow older members of the community to act as teachers and mentors to those with the same interest.

Another interest is to create a community garden so that everyone can claim a parcel of land. Here again is an opportunity to share the knowledge of gardening and meet other community members. In Lawrence County, music is a strong interest, and many citizens play instruments. This has shaped an idea to create a summer music camp for musicians to gather and learn from one another and invite guest musicians to come and share their talents. The camp would also expose children to talents within the community for possible mentorship opportunities.

Another area of interest in Lawrence County is learning the skills of canning, knitting and sewing. More people are depending on gardens to feed their families and need to know how to can their harvest. This is an opportunity to include the generation of folks who have the skills and teach those who do not. Classes are being created to teach the skills that seem to be going the way of a lost art.

"This project epitomizes the work of the Council – to create change through innovation and to develop communities where everyone belongs," CCDD Executive Director Pat Seybold said. "Council members Tina Jackson, David Minor and Donna Kouns are to be given credit for their dedication to this project. Without their time, energy and effort, this project would not have become a reality. They have truly demonstrated what can happen when a small group of people make a commitment to change a community."

*   *   *   *

I wrote the article on the next page about an activity the Louisa Community of Sharing group conducted. It appeared in a different edition of the same magazine.

BULLDOG

This article originally appeared in the Kentucky Exceptional Family Magazine and is used with permission from the Commonwealth Council on Developmental Disabilities.

If you have ever been to a Lawrence County High School football game to watch the Bulldogs play, you have no doubt seen or heard the team's biggest cheerleader and supporter, Doug Vanhoose. Doug is a Lawrence County icon. He is better known statewide as Bulldog.

Doug was born with learning difficulties and the doctors predicted a short life span, but it did not keep him from becoming a beloved, hard-working member of our community at age fifty-two.

Twenty-seven years ago, Bulldog started attending the high school football games and cheered the team from the side lines. He became such a constant fixture at games that the coach started giving him jobs to do to help the team. He carried equipment, kept the players supplied with water and towels.

Year after year he has befriended and traveled with the members of the varsity football team. Just by his presence and friendship he has taught countless young people to accept differences and a good work ethic. When you ask him what he thinks he has taught the teams, he will say he taught them respect. The coaches over the years have kept Bulldog involved with the football team and have nothing but admiration for him.

The community of sharing group decided to honor him as a valued teacher and friend to the youth in the community with a pizza party with all the coaches from over the years present to tell stories about their time with him. We gave him a framed certificate and a framed poster of a group photo to thank him for his years as a community leader.

One of the coaches told a story at the party about being at an away game and trying unsuccessfully to get through the gates to the locker rooms because he had forgot his coach's pass. They continued to try to talk their way in the gates until Bulldog came around the corner to join the coach. The guard saw Bulldog and said, "Oh are you guys with Bulldog? Go on in the gate then."

Bulldog still talks about the pizza party. One of his long-time friends, a sportswriter, suggested they make Bulldog tee shirts to sell. When asked what he would do with the proceeds, He said, "I would use it to bring people from the nursing home to home football games."

We are lucky to have Bulldog to help us celebrate the youth of our community. We all hope that he is still giving us his gifts for many years.

Bulldog is second from right on the front row.

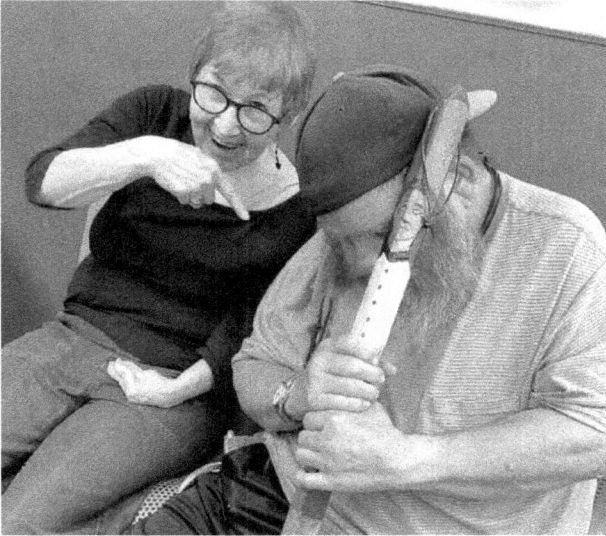

To this day, Bulldog and I remain very close friends. Here I am with him in 2025 at a local department store. He was a bit bashful.

In order to initiate the project in Louisa and become a paid employee for KYSAFF, I had to resign from the CCDD. The project started with great hopes and enthusiasm. Unfortunately, management issues and insufficient funding led to its termination after one year. I still have nightmares about the opportunity that was lost. It was very difficult for me, but it was part of my journey.

Before I left the Council, I became a member of the Leadership Circle for Self-Advocates. The Circle was established at the 2014 Annual Conference of the National Association of Councils on Developmental Disabilities (NADCC), The purpose of the Circle was to create an entry point for the many highly talented self-advocates identified by DD Councils to become more involved in the work of NACDD. As a national organization, we wanted to be sure that the voices of those who live with intellectual and developmental disabilities were included in every aspect of our work. All too often, we have found ourselves creating committees and work groups saying, "Do we have self-advocates or individuals with DD on that group?" and often the same three individuals would volunteer. By establishing the Circle, we have a ready group of highly qualified and available voices to join every committee and group within NACDD to ensure a strong advocate voice. In the first two years after its' creation, the members of this Circle helped write "The Art of Impact," served on multiple committees, and helped to pursue grant opportunities. The Leadership Circle is not a standalone committee with its own agenda, but a portal to serving in al meaningful roles in NACDD's work.

I was inducted into the National Self-Advocate Leadership Circle at an award luncheon during NACDD Annual Conference in Washington, DC, in July of 2016. I am called on from time to time to advocate for legislation or bring awareness to certain issues.

Me with my plaque from the NACDD Leadership Circle. Next to me is then-CCDD Chairperson Chastity Ross.

In 2016, I was appointed to the Protection & Advocacy for Persons with Developmental Disabilities (PADD) Board and am still serving at the time of this writing. According to the website of the agency, "Protection & Advocacy (P&A) is a federally mandated, state agency, whose mission is to protect and promote the rights of individuals who have been discriminated against due to a disability." The PADD Board advises the agency on issues related to developmental disability and is comprised of 17 individuals with a developmental disability or family members of individuals with a developmental disability.

I was appointed to the KATS Network Advisory Council in 2018. The KATS Network is the statewide assistive technology program for Kentucky. Like the CCDD and Protection and Advocacy, it receives federal funds to support its activities. The KATS Network Advisory Council provides advice and feedback to ensure that the KATS Network maintains a consumer focus. The Council consists of 14 members appointed by the Governor. As mandated by the AT Act, more than half the members of the Council must have significant disabilities.

While serving on the KATS Network Advisory Council in 2018, I heard of plans for a regular toy drive being discussed. I had a thought of a sensory toy drive because I had been talking with a high school age friend with autism on Facebook. She told me the importance of certain objects in helping calm panic such as fidget spinners, different textures, weighted lap pads or blankets. Often, the student could not afford these tools. I could imagine my father stepping up on my shoulder and whispering, "You can do this." it was his practice to help others in need without creating fanfare. I started a Facebook fundraiser and to my delight raised about $1,000.00. My friend helped me make a list of items to buy and I enlisted the skills of local ladies to make lap pads. A friend with knowledge of sensory issues shopped with me as we gathered toys. It was often an opportunity to teach the shopkeepers of the need for such toys. We took all the toys to the special education teachers just before Christmas. They were pleased to have them to distribute to the appropriate children. This could be done on a larger scale. If you are looking for a way to accommodate and comfort children with sensory disorders, this is a great way of doing it.

Most of the meetings of the KATS Network Advisory Council were in Louisville, more than three hours from our home. It was a long way for Mark to drive and we had a tough time making the trips. In addition, Mark developed some health problems. For those reasons, I decided to resign from the KATS Council in 2019.

*   *   *   *

One of my most exciting opportunities to advocate was when I was asked to say a few words at a rally led by the Reverend Dr. William Barber on June 4, 2018, in Frankfort, Kentucky, as part of the *Poor People's Campaign: A National Call for Moral Revival.* The event took place on the steps of the state Capitol and drew hundreds of Kentuckians who gathered to speak out on issues like healthcare, ecological devastation, and systemic poverty. Dr. Barber was Co-chair of the Poor People's Campaign, an effort to revive Martin Luther King Jr.'s 1968 initiative to fight poverty and systemic injustice.

Dr. Barber is a prominent American minister, social justice advocate, and public theologian known for his powerful voice in movements for racial and economic justice. He holds a Doctor of Ministry from Drew University. He was Founder of Repairers of the Breach, a nonprofit that trains communities in moral activism and an architect of the Forward Together Movement which gained national attention through "Moral Monday" protests in North Carolina. He was pastor of Greenleaf Christian Church in that state for 30 years. He has spoken at the Democratic National Convention and at President Biden's Inaugural Prayer Service.

Even more exciting that day was when Dr. Barber took my hand and gave it a sweet kiss in appreciation. I was one of many speakers that day, but I was the only one to get a sweet hand kiss. I was invited to speak as a member of Kentuckians for the Commonwealth, "a community of people building New Power and a better future for all of us." The group organizes for "a fair economy, a healthy environment, new safe energy and an honest democracy."

Here are my remarks that day:

Good afternoon. My name is Tina Jackson. I am a disability self-advocate, and member of the Kentuckians for the Commonwealth. When I learned that the Poor People's Campaign was getting a new breath of life, I was very excited. I am excited that the focus, in 2018, is truly an inclusive effort. The Poor People's March in DC in 1968 with Dr. King was mainly focused on the needs of African Americans, and rightly so.

Today we are again in a serious crossroads of danger, which could negatively impact the lives of ordinary people, be they white, disabled, black, or the working poor. We ordinary folks have a secret weapon with our votes. We can make our voices heard loudly and clearly. We need to be actively involved in recruiting candidates to run who are able to understand our need for better jobs, housing, keeping our health care intact and our environment safe, and keeping our pristine land safe from corporate greed. Then, we need to campaign for those candidates.

Martin Luther King, Jr. once said, 'we may have come over on different ships, but we are in the same boat now.' Another one of my heroes, Helen Keller, said, 'alone we can do so little, but together we can do so much.'

Thank you for allowing me this time to add my voice to this most worthy cause. Unite, include, and use your right to vote."

*　　*　　*　　*

We are all born in this world to travel different pathways through life. However, an estimated fifteen percent of us are born with a disability which can create a more difficult journey, filled with never-ending efforts to adapt and adjust to fit into a world full of obstacles and barriers, too often resulting in a shorter life span.

This is why we need to be self-advocates and support other disability advocates to work on improving inclusion, accessibility, education, healthcare, disability awareness, identifying and correcting discrimination, and supporting legislation that improves and promotes a better understanding of the needs of those who experience disabilities. There are many ways to advocate for and change the perception of people with disabilities.

One is to do the unexpected with success.

On one such occasion, I joined the Crossfit group in my town. I was the only disabled Crossfit member in the area and was pleased to find myself surrounded by a group of extremely supportive coaches and fellow Crossfitters, telling me I could do anything, and celebrating all my small achievements. I spent a year lifting weights, doing squats, cow bells and walking.

I began to notice that my routine was getting more challenging, with things like pushing giant tires and pulling a sled full of weights. I continued this routine for a month. Then one day, the coaches put a strap on me and walked me outside to where a small car was parked.

"You are going to pull this car," one coach said, smiling.

"You have to be kidding," I responded. "No way."

"You are ready!" he declared."

Armed only with my try-anything attitude and encouragement from the others, I let them strap me to the front of the car. It was the anniversary of the opening of the Louisa Crossfit, so there was a big crowd. I positioned myself in pull mode and listened to the instructions from my coaches.

The crowd roared with cheers as I took my first step. I was shocked to feel the car move. With each successive step I heard, "go Tina!" I pulled the car as far as they had intended. I felt strong and no one in the crowd saw a disabled lady; they just saw a person who had worked hard to accomplish a goal.

What I didn't realize was that I was being trained to participate in a truck pull. We went to the event in Huntington, West Virginia, and the little car was there, ready for me to pull for an even larger crowd. With the coaches by my side I pulled the car to the end of the path. I felt so elated that when I saw a truck set up to be pulled, I pointed to it and said, "I want to pull that." My coaches announced that I would attempt to do the truck, too. The crowd roared.

I took my place strapped to the truck. I started my lean and secured my footing. With my coaches bookending me I slowly moved forward with determined steps, pulling a vehicle the size of a medium U-Haul. When I arrived at the end of the lane I was met with cheers and applause. The U.S. Marines had a booth at the event and invited me over to present me with a t-shirt.

I worked hard to train for that day, to demonstrate my ability, despite having cerebral palsy and a stroke. My hope was that the people in the crowd learned not to misjudge or discount people with disabilities, just by appearances. That lesson would only be learned by performing these feats in the public, in front of people with all abilities. Inclusion is the window into acceptance.

Pulling the truck

*　　*　　*　　*

In 2021, just before the Lawrence County Fair in Louisa, I learned it was situated on a hillside, making it impossible for people with disabilities or older people to enjoy the events or vending booths. It was located at 545 Pine Hill Road and that name isn't just poetic. The fairgrounds are on elevated terrain, with parts of the venue sloping gently across the property. If you've ever felt like you were walking uphill between booths or noticed vendors perched at different heights, you weren't imagining it. This hilly layout adds a bit of charm to the fair, especially during outdoor events like the rodeo or livestock shows. But if you're planning to visit or set up a booth, it's worth considering the terrain for accessibility and visibility.

After learning from other people with children who were in wheelchairs that the paths were covered with large gravel that wheelchairs could not travel over, I went to the fair board and the county judge to make them aware of the accessibility problem. They countered with, "We have a shuttle from the parking lot," but not even the shuttle was accessible. I tried to talk to the county judge, but we come to an agreement on the issue. I tried to arrange a meeting with the fair board and ADA

112

officials, but could not. No changes have been made to the fairgrounds, to my understanding. I have been told that changing the fairgrounds would be too expensive.

This was ironic since the county was presented a grant to construct an accessibility playground in Lawrence in 2020. Governor Andy Beshear announced a $50,000 Recreational Trails Program (RTP) grant to Lawrence County Fiscal Court to add an accessible playground and splash park in Lawrence County Park. As of the date of this writing, only one accessible swing has been placed the park. I have spoken to the county judge about it. One swing does not make the playground accessible.

Mark and I with Kentucky Governor Andy Beshear when he was in town to announce the accessible playground grant.

A Warm Day in December

When I tire of the winter's cold,
And spring is hard to remember
When things look bleak and old,
God sends a warm day in December.

Inspired by a new start for us all!

The wind blew by my window today,
And told of many things.
It said the sun was on its way,
And little blue birds on new wings.

It puffed and puffed and made a breeze,
That soothed this tired, old soul.
It crooned a tune that rustled the trees,
And reminded me to take an evening stroll.

A robin danced in my front yard today,
She hopped and hopped and flew into a tree.
She's returned to this familiar place to stay,
It's her old nesting spot she's come to see.

Dandelions grew in my yard this week,
With a bright yellow hue,
It made me smile just to think,
Last week I felt so blue.

The wind blew by my window today,
And told me of a glorious new spring,
It blew and blew, as if to say,
Come join me in these gifts from the King.

Chapter 13

A Remembrance of My Mentor, Sarah

I have always wished to be a time traveler so I could answer questions I often ponder. How did people live in other times? What were the factors influencing their daily lives? How different would my life be if I'd been born in another era?

Fifteen years ago, I became acquainted with a bright, articulate, elderly lady from South Carolina. Through our frequent conversations and correspondence, she shared with me a detailed description of how life was for a young, single female in the South during the 30's and 40's.

My friend was "Miss Sarah." She was also known affectionately as Tata because one of her young nephews could not pronounce Sarah. She was lovingly called that the rest of her life.

Sarah was born into a wealthy family. Her father was a doctor and a strong figure in their small, rural community. Many of her uncles were prominent attorneys and physicians. Her mother, a prim and proper lady of the house, died when Sarah was only six years old.

After the death of her mother, nannies and house staff raised Sarah and her older sister, Julia. Sarah and Julia were expected to take on the role of ladies of the house and hostesses for their father's guests. They also acted as mothers to the younger siblings. Sarah never questioned her role or examined her own goals. Her future was determined by her family's needs. In the society of the time, women were expected to hold the family structure together.

Education was stressed in the upper middle classes of South Carolina. Sarah got her education from a religious college for teachers. Teaching and performing charity work were two of the acceptable ways women could spend their time outside the home in those days. Sarah worked part time because it was the only way single women could work and still be "proper." Even though Sarah would have liked to do more beyond her family obligations, it was not permitted.

She loved to travel, though it was not proper for a single woman to travel alone. However, it was respectable to go on mission trips with church groups, so Sarah took every opportunity to do so. She traveled extensively, from Alaska to the hills of Kentucky, teaching reading or instructing young mothers in childcare. It was good and proper for women to use their education for God's will. Sarah loved doing this work and it fed her soul.

When members of the family became ill or were dying, Sarah was called upon to care for them, because she was single. Without regard to her own needs and desires, Sarah cared for several dying relatives. She considered it an honor to put her family first. This kind of selfless reasoning has practically evaporated in our current society.

Although Sarah's family, church, and the society at large dictated how she lived her life, she often displayed an independent nature. When she drove her car, she drove fast. I believe getting in her car alone gave her a sense of autonomy and solitude that she rarely experienced and she took full advantage of these opportunities to exercise her freedom.

Another act of strong independence surfaced when Sarah witnessed the needs of the black children of the farm hands in her community. This was the 1940s, a period of intense prejudice in the deep south. Everything was segregated, but the children had a place to learn the Bible. Her family farm was expansive and contained several abandoned cabins. Sarah utilized one of the cabins to open a Sunday school for the black children. This was revolutionary for the time but was deemed a proper act of charity because she was teaching religion and it did not involve the white parishioners. She could not nor would not ask for assistance from the church.

Sarah taught in the public school system until she learned that part of her salary was derived from the sales tax of alcohol products. She promptly resigned, feeling that her values and morals were being compromised. She returned to charity and mission work. The influence of the church was strong, due to the fact that the church was the hub of community activity as well as for worship and religious education. People met there to plan community events, gather socially, and make important decisions.

The population of Sarah's community was not transient, as it often is today. Remarkably, Sarah maintained deep, intimate friendships for more than seventy years, with people from her childhood, college, and church. I feel lucky to have even one friend since 4th grade! Sarah trusted and relied on her community to help in times of need. Living with the same people for seventy years must create bonds as strong as steel.

Sarah lived her life in the manner she felt her family, church, and society expected of her. The time she did spend on her own projects was made possible by her family's wealth. Her father gave her his full support.

When I last spoke with "Miss Sarah," she was still questioning herself and her motives. Did she do all God wanted her to do with the time He gave her? Did she make unselfish choices in her decision-making process? It is difficult for me to believe that she still doubts her worth in this world.

When I'm eighty-five, I hope my life reflects good deeds. I hope I'm still questioning my motives, as Sarah did. For it's in this way that I may see all paths open to me and make unselfish choices.

I regret to say that I lost my good friend not long ago. She knew that her time on earth was short, and she gifted me with some of the books from her personal library and a set of

China. I am so blessed to have known her. Barring my ability to time travel, I look forward to seeing her again. We'll have a long chat.

Tata Sarah

With You Still

From the impetuous girl,
grew the careful woman,
Her lonely silence,
has closed her soul.

Once warm and open,
now cold and sullen,
She is well rehearsed,
in her new role.

The girl danced,
till her song,
could no longer play.

Gone is the music,
that gave her the dance.
This girl, this woman,
who live as one,
are here to stay.

These two,
one up,
one down,
still have a chance.

The music is with her,
in a dream,
From the lonely heart,
and silent soul,
a voice still does cry,

To mold together,
this perfect team.
It brings the comfort,
and strength to try.

It's a voice
that helps this tired,
sad woman's soul to heal,

For it is the voice,
of the impetuous girl,
that cries,
"I'm here!
I am here!
I am with you still!"

Chapter 14

The Fight Never Ends

I began the new Millennium needing additional assistance due to the progression of my cerebral palsy and post-stroke central nervous system damage which caused more anxiety and more vision and balance problems. I use a small cart to help with my balance, which allows me to continue being ambulatory and active in the community.

At this point in my life, I am able to answer a question that I asked myself as a disabled child: "what happens to people with cerebral palsy when they get old?" As a 63-year-old born with cerebral palsy and who had a stroke at 24, I can tell that young girl that it's going to be okay. You can handle all the challenges put to you in your life. I got old, but I was able to earn two degrees, and work as long as my body allowed. The stroke took my speech, but I still attended college as someone who could not talk, and worked for AT&T for years. I would tell that young girl that she will be blessed with parents who allowed her to try anything she desires. This gives you strength and builds independence that you will need when you fall, and when you will fall, you will get up and try again. Learning from your mistakes and doing it better the next time is a factor in growing older.

I can't remember when it all started, this feeling of being old. I had always looked younger than my age. Though distressing for an adolescent who wanted to look mature, it gave me a secret pleasure at 30, to be mistaken for a minor when out with my peers.

I had conquered the physical demands of the years that I walked the college campus with a six-pound bag of books on my shoulder. There were the years I conquered anxiety and fear to make the six-hour drive to North Carolina alone every other month. I made the trek to my job through downtown Cincinnati while battling panic attacks and the dread of crowds and crossing streets.

Then, one day, not long ago, I turned a corner and walked by a storefront window. I thought, "Who is that old lady?" I was shocked to realize it was my own reflection. Me, the little freckled face kid, the teenager who desperately wanted to look more mature, the woman who was secretly delighted by her youthful look.

Like I said, I can't really remember when it all started, this feeling of being old, but I was old, no doubt about it. Things I encountered every day became more challenging. Curbs were difficult to navigate because I'd lose my balance. One day as I washed my face, I saw a terrain of lines and wrinkles. I don't know when they appeared, but there they were on a face that once fooled everyone. Now I had a face to match the body; a body that's slowly losing energy and function. Youth is no longer my ally to help fight the battles.

Even though the years have blurred together and I didn't notice when I got my gray hair, wrinkles, and a general feeling that my best years of life were over, I rejoice in the knowledge that my time in this earthly body is not the end. I know that my eternal body will be a perfect vessel. I've been presented with extraordinary challenges and, perhaps, old age before my time, because it's helped me appreciate what I have, and to strive to do my best with what God gave me.

Despite my added challenges, I continued to be an active volunteer at my church. I led a historical committee and co-wrote the history of the church, as well as contributing a monthly item for the church newsletter. I use a text reader on my computer to read long articles and edit my writing.

I have always understood that as I age, my body and mind will degenerate somewhat faster than the ordinary person. I know I will experience a variety of losses. My independence will be impacted in ways that will change my lifestyle and even how I understand my world.

I think about the aspects of independence I can lose and the ones I have already lost due to aging with cerebral palsy. I fear losing more mobility, my memory, my active social life, and the ability to make decisions, perform daily activities, and do disability advocacy.

After a fall on Christmas Eve in 2022 resulting in two fractures to my pelvis, my existing independence was severely threatened. When I got to the emergency room with my niece, before any assessment or x-ray, the doctor's first words were, "So are we looking for a nursing home placement?" as he looked at my niece. Going to a nursing home was my greatest fear because I knew that with this type of fracture at my age, nursing home was a typical result.

My niece said absolutely not. The doctor would not admit me to the hospital for assessment. I went home not being able to walk, go to the bathroom or feed myself. I went back to ER the next day, hoping for more help. Again, the doctor would not admit me even after discovering I had not just one but two breaks and was in a great deal of pain. My family contacted a family friend who is a doctor and he called the ER and instructed them to admit me in his name. I began to see the light. I was admitted and approved for two weeks of intensive physical therapy.

The first day I could not bear weight on my left leg. I was given pain medicine and the next day I took my first steps. I was belted for safety, but I took three steps forward and three backward to the bed. My emotions took over and I started to cry. For a few days, my mind had been mourning the loss of life as I knew it. Standing in the hospital, I began giving thanks to God and everyone who helped me get admitted.

I had therapy twice a day, standing longer, taking more steps, and envisioning my future back in my little house. The nurses and aides celebrated every success: walking to the chair, feeding myself with my feeding tube stand, dressing. On my last day in the hospital, I walked almost 500 feet with ease.

The threats to my independence still linger out there and I know I have many more in my path. but I won this battle with hard work and determination. I plan to meet each challenge and threat in the same fashion.

I will not allow doctors, or anyone, to assume my ability or worth!

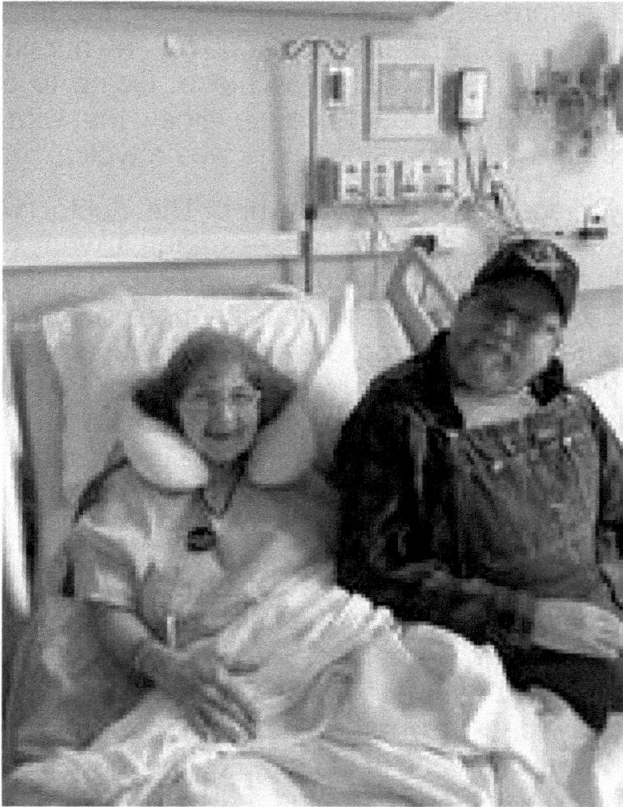

Mark and me in the hospital during my recovery.

*   *   *   *

What can one person do to influence change in this very scary world of politics? I was raised by parents who were very active in the community and my father was active with union negotiations on his job. So it came easy for me to get involved in women's rights movement in my late teens traveling to DC twice for protests in support of the Equal Rights Amendment (ERA). The ERA was a proposed amendment to the U.S. Constitution that aimed to explicitly prohibit sex discrimination. It was first introduced in 1923 and gained momentum in the 70's during the women's movement.

As I aged my cerebral palsy created more limitations and I was in need of additional resources and an accessible environment. I found both were lacking. Resources that I and many others need to live at home are not being funded adequately and even though the Americans with Disabilities Act (ADA) was passed there are many places that are still not accessible to me and others like me.

A most recent concern to me as I write this in the spring of 2025 is the very real possibility of cuts to Medicaid. Cuts to Medicaid would severely threaten my independence. I might not be able to afford my feeding tube formula. My ability to engage with my community could be curtailed. My in-home assistance might be reduced as well as my transportation. The general quality of my life could be greatly affected.

Protests have played a crucial role in shaping policy decisions over the years. Activists have successfully influenced lawmakers by staging sit-ins, disrupting congressional hearings, and organizing large-scale demonstrations. Living in a rural area limits my ability to participate in rallies now so I advocate how I am able. Yes, I am just one voice, but I have faith that joined with other voices I am heard and seen.

In April of 2025, Mark and I staged our own mini-protest against possible Medicaid cuts in the streets of Ashland. It was just the two of us in our scooters joined by a friend. We got a lot of attention – thumbs up, horn beeps, nods. One man even prayed with us. The guard at the Social Security Office was very nice to us. Unfortunately, we got rained out after two hours. But we had to do something. We had to make our voices heard. My advocacy will never end.

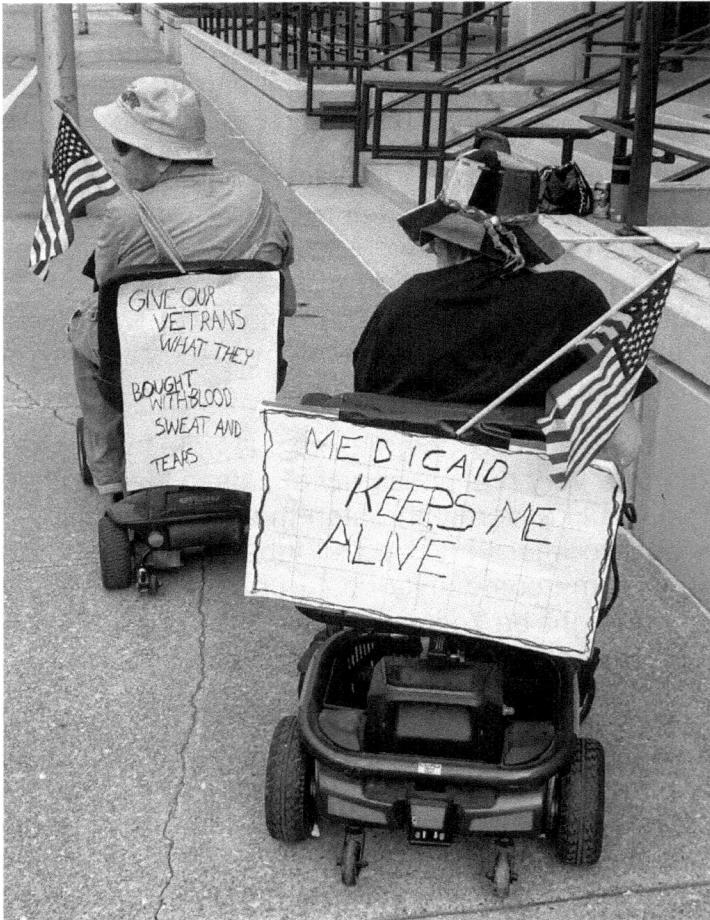

Protesting Medicaid cuts

I want to be this person!

Forgive me if my walk is slow
This life was not my plan
There's much you don't know
I do the best I can

You see me drop or spill
I feel your lingering stare
Don't think me mentally ill
Just show a bit of care

I am now gray and old
This life was not my plan
I see a girl strong and bold
I do the best I can

Chapter 15
Some Final Reflections

When I decided to try and write my story, it was in the hopes of encouraging people to overcome obstacles by setting goals and using the right resources to live a successful and productive life. I can tell you how I accomplished many of my goals and contributed to society, but the story would not be complete, and I'd be a hypocrite, if I didn't talk about the dark side of living with a disability.

Even though I was born with mild cerebral palsy and experienced a debilitating stroke, I lived a very independent life until age forty. At that time, my body would not allow me to continue driving, eating as most people eat, or working a traditional job. The drastic, painful leap from needing no help to having to depend on others to participate in society spiraled my once high self-esteem into depression and ignited my most challenging disability, anxiety. I developed irrational fears of being alone and my mobility was severely hampered by fears of falling.

Losing my speech further complicated my ability to take part in activities. When trying to communicate, it often ended in frustration when I was talked over or unable to use my communication devices in noisy rooms. I have lost the art of conversation. It makes me very sad, because I genuinely enjoyed a spontaneous chat. That is no longer possible.

I can explain better by taking you through one of my typical days. My morning commences with hooking up to a feeding tube for breakfast and medications. This includes a process of crushing my medicines to insert into the tube. The medications often clog the tube, and the unclogging is messy and exasperating. I pour my liquid nutrition down the tube. Aspiration is a common event, leading to coughing and spilling. Then I need to sit still for thirty minutes to avoid spitting up my food.

Not only did I lose the ability to eat due to my stroke, I can no longer swallow saliva. Constant drooling is demeaning and embarrassing. I use medication to dry out my saliva when in public. However, people do see me dribble, negatively influencing their perception of me and not seeing me as the smart, capable, and accomplished person I know myself to be. When I'm home or with family I insert a paper towel to stop the flow.

My days are now consumed with panic attacks if I go out. Anxiety affects me so much more than my cerebral palsy ever did. I never know when I'll suddenly freeze in fear of some unknown danger. At these inopportune times I need to be walked to a safe place.

Another source of frustration is dressing for the day; with one hand it used to be easy. As I age, I get slower and sometimes need help from Mark. Simple tasks have become harder.

I fight to stay strong and as independent as possible. The battle is tiresome.

I have to plan my day carefully to allow for meals and medications. I have to arrange for a ride if I need to go anywhere. What I would not give to hop in my car, turn up the music, and take a drive as I did in my younger days!

I can no longer sleep in a bed because it causes backache and pulls on my tube site. So, my day ends in my recliner next to Mark in his recliner.

Sometimes I feel badly for Mark. When we married twenty-three years ago, he didn't bargain on becoming a caretaker, but that's what has happened. He is now my driver, my interpreter, and the person who takes care of the house and dog. He encourages my participation in my disability advocacy work, which continues to be my avenue to feeling active and involved in the world.

I miss the life I had with all its freedoms, but I must accept the life I have now. I will use the tools I've always had to move on after countless setbacks and restarts. I will set new goals. I will continue to fight the negative self-thoughts which have led me to think of suicide in several periods in my life. I will continue to stand up for social justice causes, campaign for candidates who support my views, and speak up for and about disability issues.

*   *   *   *

The wiser mind mourns less for what age takes away than what it leaves behind." — William Wordsworth

One of the things I am most proud of about my life is the work I have done to live a very independent lifestyle. It took a multi-level process of planning from childhood. My parents made sure I learned to do housework, lawn care, gardening, laundry, cooking, money management, drive and maintain a car. It took searching out support systems and learning job skills through higher education after choosing career paths. I forged friendships with people who could help guide my path. I consulted with vocational rehabilitation field counselors when I needed more support in obtaining employment. I was successful in my quest to live independently for many years.

I am 69 now as I write this. There was a time when I feared I would not live to age 40. I have traveled my path in life with unusual ease, considering my entrance into the world was traumatic and my future and my abilities were a complete unknown. I went through each stage and change with determination and planning. My infancy and childhood were filled with a happy family and parents who supported my needs, involving me in physical therapy and early education classes at the age of two, preparing me for the future, which was pretty much unknown. I was able to enter regular school through college, earning two degrees.

Life continued as I was gainfully employed for years. My social life included many friends with whom I have kept friendships for over forty years. I lived alone until I married at 42. I loved being able to do whatever I wanted. I drove where I pleased. I was happy in my little world. I think of how I could jump in my Chevy Nova, two-toned tans, turn on the radio, slip on my cool shades, and visit, shop, go to class, see a movie, I could drive to North Carolina periodically to visit family or Cincinnati to listen to my friend play in her band or to a high point to catch the sunset. I even did something I never dreamed I would ever do. I got married at 42.

It was at this point that my body began to change. I was still working full time and driving, but I became fatigued easily, and my mobility worsened. My outings became filled with anxiety and unpleasant. Driving was scary. When I would go out anxiety took control, and I would often fall when in open spaces. I decided to end traditional employment as the days of 8 hours on the job left me sick and weak. It was the end of the life I had built with determination and grit. But it would not be the last change in my life. I had been through many changes, and many more would come. Tests revealed I would require a feeding tube for the rest of my life to avoid aspiration pneumonia. So began my later years of life at only 42. My body would not allow me to do housework because it caused back pain. I took the first step to get help by applying for a Medicaid Home and Community Waiver for housework and groceries. This was a suitable solution for the time, and I also acquired a power chair to aid me in mobility. At age 69, I needed more care, so I am now using a daily care aide, along with my husband, who also requires an aide.

These are big changes to our home lifestyle. It is up to us how we allow these changes to redirect our lives and help us set new goals, regain activity in the community, and view it as a move forward. It is depressing to redefine my identity.

When I interviewed people to be my caretaker, I asked a question that I could not imagined myself asking before. I asked, "Do you have experience with elder care?"

*   *   *   *

Very great change starts from very small conversations, held among people who care. *- Margaret J. Wheatley*

I can be a very lonely person, but I do not admit that to many people. My favorite memories are starting a conversation at bus stops, laundromats, or restaurants. Making a new friend always made my day. I took immense pride in my ability to converse with anyone. Losing my voice is not just physical but also social, emotional, and lonely. Being nonverbal changed my thought processes, as I must respond before the other party got tired of waiting and walk away. I must condense my responses thus becoming less meaningful and complete. Conversations become one-sided and fragmented. I still think clearly, but my ability to express those thoughts has become laborious and trapped in silence. I often find myself sitting alone at social gatherings. such as church events.

The effort it takes to talk with me when I am using my communication device is too great and people walk away. It requires time, patience, and effort to sit and converse with me with my speech device or Sign language.

I do not speak in the traditional sense. But I converse with words to, challenge assumptions, and dialogue with history. My advocacy is a conversation with the future with systemic insight—exactly the kind of writing that leaves a legacy of advocacy.

An enjoyable conversation is a dance, not a monologue. When both parties engage, ask questions, and listen. Nonverbal does not mean voiceless. It means we speak in ways the world must learn to hear.

Although I will never have the form of verbal interaction that I loved. I have learned that this can happen without speaking. I can even be funny! By writing, advocacy, the concept of "roaring" in conjunction with other "voices", I can be heard. Letters, texts, poetry, memoir and Sign language, facial expressions, body language and assistive technology. I have learned the art of conversation is not gone for me, but it has, taken a new evolution through technology and body language

*   *   *   *

Whatever affects one directly, affects all indirectly. I can never be what I ought to be until you are what you ought to be. This is the interrelated structure of reality. - <u>Martin Luther King, Jr.</u>

Independence can be a wonderful feeling of freedom and empowerment, but it can also be a harmful and rigid state of mind that robs the disabled the opportunity to ask for help. Independence is achieved after a long hard battle and becomes part of a person's identity. According to society, I was a success, and I did not want to let go of that identity or be thought of as a failure or weak.

When it became undeniable that, in order to keep my quality of life that I had worked so hard to achieve and maintain, I had to seek out resources for help. Help is a word I had avoided. I took pride in in my autonomy. Living with a lifelong disability and struggling to do all I needed done led me to deep depression and frustration. There was a shame I felt for asking for help.

After a lot of prayer and self-examination of my life and accomplishments, it was time I adjusted my thoughts. I redefined my idea of self and added a novel word to my vocabulary - interdependent. I learned what it meant to be interdependent. It is an actual movement within the disability justice community. It emphasizes the idea that we all rely on each other to create inclusion. It takes the focus off the individual and puts it on the barriers around them.

133

I now challenge the myth that independence equals strength. Interdependence is not weakness—it's wisdom. We in the disability community thrive through connection, creativity, and collective care. True inclusion means designing a world where support is celebrated, not hidden.

It is the perfect way to use my new voice. I used to think independence was the goal. That needing help meant I was falling short. But I've come to see that my voice—though nonverbal—is amplified through others. Through technology, through allies, through systems that listen. I am not less because I rely on support. I am more because I know how to build bridges. My story isn't about standing alone. It is about standing together. It has been my experience that exposure is the greatest teacher. The people who come in my home to help me have expressed that Mark and I are the first disabled people they have met in a meaningful way. They have also learned the difference between independence and interdependence. It has been a powerful way to advocate disability awareness. Plus, I am able to stay active in my community.

I plan to volunteer at a nearby children's hospital in the future. It's a goal I have had for a long time. I could not do this without my aide. Children love to learn Sign language. I think it would be a good distraction from being sick.

Chapter 16

The Power and Necessity of Youth in Disability Advocacy

"Disability only becomes a tragedy when society fails to provide the things we need to live our lives." - Judy Heuman

As you turn the last pages of this book, I hope that you have a better understanding of disability and disability advocacy, which is not only important but also essential.

The job of advocacy means you learn to roar alongside many other disabled voices. You can help tear down walls of exclusion, demand that society see disability not as a limitation, but as a strength, and when disabled voices are not heard, humankind is in danger. This is true now more than at any other time in history with fewer leaders who do understand or listen to the concerns that are hurting millions of disabled citizens and children.

History proves the power of advocacy. The Americans with Disabilities Act, and similar victories worldwide, were not gifts—they were won through relentless activism. Every ramp, every caption, every accessible workplace is a testament to voices that refused to be ignored as advocates.

I began my own advocacy journey by living a life that was a witness to others that having cerebral palsy did not mean I could not be in college, be employed, and drive and live alone. My formal experience as a disability justice fighter started with serving on state disability councils such as the Council for Developmental Disabilities, the Council for Vocational Rehabilitation, and Protection and Advocacy for Individuals with Developmental Disabilities Council. This is where I learned how to keep track of legislation dealing with the disabled, how to prepare for talking to lawmakers in my region, and how to help give a voice to those who cannot speak for themselves and keeping them safe.

Advocacy must continue. Join me in this work. My years as an advocate have been so rewarding. I know that I have made a difference in altering society's prejudice toward the disabled. I will never stop trying to improve the quality of life for all, but we need fresh ideas. We need a movement!

I ask young people to convey fresh energy and creativity to advocacy. Your voices can reshape policies, schools, and communities. There are many ways to be active in the justice movement:

- Be the ally who listens, amplifies, and stands beside.
- Be the community leader who organizes movements that change laws.
- Be the policymaker who ensures inclusive legislation in written in every part of society.

Each voice matters. It is about making sure everyone has the chance to speak for themselves. You can advocate in many nontraditional ways, too.

Remain observant wherever you find places in your community that are barriers for people in wheelchairs and older folks. This could be the workplace, public buildings, or broken sidewalks.

Identify discrimination and inaccessibility to housing. As I wrote earlier in this book, one of my experiences with prejudices came when my husband and I went to talk to the local realtor to discuss buying a house I saw for sale. The moment two disabled people entered his office he assumed that we could never afford a house. It took my mother to convince him that we could definitely afford it. He must have done some research on us. We are well known in my town as very productive and capable people because on our next visit to his office he was very humble. He made the purchase go faster than most. We changed his view of the disabled, I hope

Another example was the placement of the county fair. It was located on the side of a hill making it totally impossible for chairs or a stroller to access the booths. I made the fair board aware of this situation with no success. Sometimes, your efforts are not going to have a successful conclusion but I told my story to every official I could and I will not stop speaking up if I see something that needs to be changed. This is an example that you can connect with families and local groups to address these needs. Local groups are likely to rally around a clear, tangible need.

Another non-traditional way I advocate is to try to humanize being different. I use a feeding tube to get my nutrition. Whenever I eat in public it always gets looks from people who have never seen an unusual way to eat. Sometimes it sparks conversations about disabilities, and they tell stories of family members who are living a life with differences. Once on a cruise ship I was bombarded with questions from the staff who were from countries who thought the disabled should not be seen. By the end of the cruise, they had a new idea of the disabled. We belong everywhere!

Some first steps to being an effective disability advocate are getting to know your senator and state representative in your district. They want to hear from their constituents. Get to know the leaders in your community and school. These people are valuable tools for the work of an advocate.

My goal is to help to develop a society where disability is a valued identity, not a barrier. Youth advocacy can lead to more inclusive policies and accessible environments. Empowered young leaders can ensure disability rights are central to the justice movement. Your voice matters, your story matters. Do not stop telling it. We need a movement to carry on this work crucial to the lives of all people who share this space in the world. Roar with me. Advocacy is the heartbeat of justice.

"Disability is an opportunity for innovation. When we design for accessibility, everyone benefits." - **Haben Girma (first deafblind graduate of Harvard Law School)**

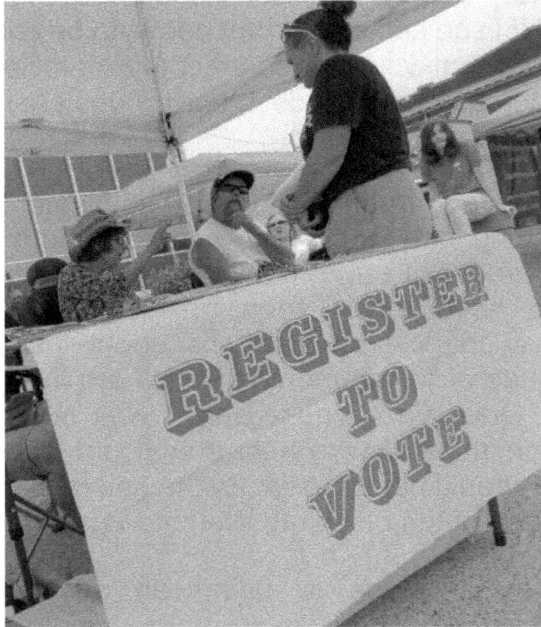

Mark and I registering people to vote.

Appendix A:
My Speech to Employees of the Kentucky Office of Vocational Rehabilitation, 2010

Thank you very much for giving me the opportunity today to share some of my experiences with the Kentucky Office of Vocational Rehabilitation. For me this a special honor because I have known quite a few staff members from this agency during my thirty year off and on relationship with the OVR and have maintained friendships and communications with several people over these many years.

My life has been a succession of new and unique disabilities, which has made it necessary for me to make contact with the people at Vocational Rehabilitation, at different times in my life, for assistance in maintaining my independence.

I was born in the 1950's with cerebral palsy resulting in the limited use of my left side. At that time, and even as a teenager, there were very few resources available for the physically challenged concerning career counseling. Therefore, I did not receive much help in that respect in public school and I remember feeling very anxious about my future all through high school.

On one occasion in school, I did attempt to talk about my interest in library science to someone whom I thought could advise me. However, it was never encouraged nor addressed other than to tell me I was not able to do that job.

God blessed me with parents who taught me the significane of independence, hard work and education, so, I recognized and appreciated the value of these things, but sadly, I did not have the self-confidence to apply them toward a practical life goal I really believed I could accomplish.

After finishing high school with average grades, I had an unsuccessful year of college at Morehead State and found myself back home with my parents feeling all the more, as though I was drifting, without purpose, lost and somewhat less then smart. It seemed to me as though I had very few options left.

At that time, all that was evident to me was that I very much wanted to find a way to support myself with employment, but I did not know what jobs were within my abilities. Without any proper job skills, employers quickly rejected me when going on job interviews. However, the tides of change were shifting my favor with the passage of the Rehabilitation Act of 1973, which paved the way for the 1990 Americans with Disabilities Act (ADA).

I became aware of vocational rehabilitation services in 1975, when friend suggested that I meet with Wade Bailey, the local field counselor for the Kentucky VR. He said something very meaningful to an unsure, worried teenager looking for answers and eased the anxiety about the future. He said that one bad year of college at 17 did not make me less smart and that many young people are not ready for college directly after leaving high school. He explained there were alternative ways to accomplish my employment goals such as vocational training.

Shortly thereafter, I entered the Carl D. Perkins Comprehensive Rehabilitation Center for evaluation. By the way, the name change to Vocational Training Center is very helpful for me and my fellow graduates' resumes.

The two-week evaluation process at the Perkins Center not only tested my intelligence, my physical abilities, my social skills but also my ability to make a serious life goal and commit to accomplishing it. While at the center, I gained the skills and confidence to concentrate my efforts toward a goal for employment and overcome individual limitations to find a lifestyle that would give me the greatest satisfaction.

You will never guess what the conclusion was from all my evaluations---go back to college!

Appendix B:

My Speech to the 2011 Graduating Class of the Carl D. Perkins Vocational Training Center

Executive Director Smith, Commissioner Brinly, parents, teachers, family, and friends. Welcome and thank you very much for joining us today to pay tribute to the graduating class of 2011 from the Carl D. Perkins Training Center and to celebrate the beginning of many new paths that will be forged in the future by this group of new graduates. I have been asked to say a few words to you today because some time ago, we will not say how long, I sat where you are sitting today. I am very excited for you because I know that the world is open to motivated people like you who have the fortitude and desire to make your life a success on the path in which you choose to forge.

By completing your chosen course at the training center and sitting here today, you have taken the fundamental first step in the effort to making your life happy and successful. The success that I am speaking of here today has nothing to do with money or fame, rather it is measured by happiness and the satisfaction of knowing you have made every effort to become the person you desire to be.

Success is a lifelong journey. It is not just the accomplishment of a single goal but an ongoing series of accomplishments on your path that will result in major achievements in life. However, this graduation is just one of many steps that will be necessary to achieve the goals that you set for yourself. Setting goals is the only way you can move forward in a purposeful way. Setting a goal helps you to bridge the gap between where you are now and where you want to be. A proper goal gives you all the incentive that you need to grow in your awareness of what you want and how to do it. It commits you to achieving it. If you have not done so already, begin planning for your future tonight. If you are not happy with the path your life has taken so far, change it or blaze your own trail if you need to, but take this excellent opportunity to use the resources given to you by the training center and make the most of it. This is the reason we came to this center. We needed to gain the skills and confidence to concentrate our efforts toward a better future and overcome our individual limitations to find our way to a job and lifestyle that will give us the greatest satisfaction.

Your goals may change over time, but the amount of hard work will be constant throughout life. After I left the center with my set of new skills, I forged the first of many new paths I am not the traditional person. It was difficult at times however it was very exciting and satisfying in ways no traditional person can understand because achieving a goal takes much more work and dedication as it will for many of you, but the rewards of seeing your labor conclude at the realization of a dream are immeasurable.

I thought that by going to college earning a degree and working as a social worker would be my life until I had a stroke. I had to regroup, set new goals, learn new job skills. I took the office administration course here at the Center and went to work for a Fortune 500 company in Cincinnati. I thought that I would be there until retirement until I was laid off six years later. Again I had to regroup, set new goals and learn new job skills. I did and worked in the health information field until my physical condition failed after five years on the job and I became dependent on the feeding tube. All my efforts to stay independent and employed which were my goals had to carry on in spite of my new limitations, but in a different way.

My husband Mark and I developed an assistive device for the feeding tube dependent because it was so beneficial to me and there were no other device like it on the market. We received a patent for it and we are now selling the product to others in my situation. I never thought I would ever be a small business owner, but that was the path I had to forge to retain my sense of purpose. It took years and years of product development research and hard work to receive the patents, get the product on the market and see any results. However, the reward of seeing the device help others to maintain their independence is worth the long, long days and nights of work and searching out resources.

If you hear and take away with you anything I say today, I hope that it is you are capable of accomplishing any goal if you are flexible and stay focused. You may have to be creative and teach the world to adapt to your abilities, but we who are not traditional people are excellent teachers of patience, acceptance, respect, and tolerance. We are excellent workers because we know the value of independence.

I encourage you to surround yourself with supportive people. Remember your parents, your teachers and loved ones who have stood by you thus far and include them in your life. We all need people in our lives to encourage us, advise us, and give us confidence through the difficult times. Go out and set your goals, find your passion, work hard, and shine your special light on the world. It is waiting for talented, interesting, capable, hard-working people to contribute to making this country and this world a little better place for us all. God bless you all as you each go your own way. Be good teachers, good workers, good role models, and a good friend. As anything you do in life, you will get out as much as you are willing to put into achieving happiness and success. I would like to leave you with an inspiring quote from Norman Vincent Peale, "Shoot for the moon. Even if you miss, you'll land among the stars."

Have a wonderful day!

Appendix C:
My Grandparents Elope
Taken from an article I wrote for the
Kentucky Explorer Magazine

In the spring of 1928, my grandmother Ethel Porter, 16, was living in Ashland, Kentucky, with her parents and seven brothers. They had moved there from their home in Bruin, KY, which is on the county line of Carter and Elliott Counties. Her father, James Porter was doing construction work in Ashland helping to build the Ashland train depot. While living in Ashland that spring she became acquainted with my grandfather, Albert Blevins, then 21, who had also moved to Ashland from rural Carter county to work at Armco Steel a year or two before. Albert was living with his sister, Dessy, in a house not far from Ethel. During their courtship they would go to see movies at the Capital Theater in Ashland or sit in Ethel's parents' parlor and listen to shows like Grand Ol' Opry on the radio.

When the work at the Ashland depot was finished the Porter family moved back to Bruin to the country home. On the farm, Ethel would work taking care of the housework, doing laundry on a scrub board with homemade lye soap. With seven brothers, this task seemed endless. She helped tend to the chickens, cows, and hogs on the farm. These animals gave them the basics of milk, eggs, pork and beef. It also gave them bartering power to acquire salt, sugar, pepper, lard, and coffee. Eggs were traded for these things at the store. The family would use the herb bonset to make cough syrup, dandelion root was used for kidney aliments and pine solvin for wounds.

The courtship of Ethel and Albert continued through letters and occasional visits by Albert to Ethel in Bruin. This was not a trip around the corner. To see his new love, Albert made an all day journey that started by taking a bus from Ashland to Grayson. Then, he would catch the "Blue Goose", a small passenger train which ran to several small towns along the Ohio River, to Willard. He then walked over the hill to Beetle, KY where he could get a horse to ride on to Bruin. Today this trip would take less than an hour in a car. This arrangement of letters and visits went on for a couple of months before Albert devised a plan to have Ethel with him forever.

On May 16, 1928, my grandmother told her mother that she was going to walk to the general store with her girlfriend, Annie Blevins, who was Albert's cousin. She said she would be right back with some cigarettes for her brother, Cecil. She and Annie walked two to three miles to a large hay field where Albert was waiting for her with a preacher, the Rev. H. Wilcox and two witnesses, friend Roy Wright and cousin Emmett Blevins. Roy had secured horses to make their escape after they were wed.

Everything would have gone off without a hitch except that Annie feared for herself if she kept the secret. She walked back to alert the Porter family of the nuptials taking place down the road. Ethel knew that Annie had told the family when standing in the field after the ceremony, she could hear her mother's voice from over the hill calling for her brother Cecil.

From the wedding, the couple rode horses to the train station in Willard to start the all day trip back to Ashland. Ethel took nothing with her so as not to arouse suspicion. Cecil was waiting for them. Because she was so young, he had been sent by the family to bring Ethel home. However, after he saw proof that a marriage did take place, he relented and the couple was allowed to board the "Blue Goose." Ethel would not return to Bruin or her family except for occasional visits. Both families came to accept the union right away.

Ethel and Albert moved in with Albert's brother in Ashland. My grandparents lived in Ashland since 1928. They raised ten children and remained married until Albert's death in 1992.

Acknowledgements

I would like to acknowledge some individuals who have helped me with this project. First, I want to thank Dave Matheis for all of his help in putting this book together. Second, thanks to Susan Brown and Melanie Palombi for contributing to the cover design and to Hannah Richards for the final design. And thanks to Lee Corman and Sarah Richardson for proofreading the book.

Thanks to my oldest sister, Elizabeth, who read the book as I was writing it and encouraged me, adding memories throughout the process. My biggest fan.

Most of all, I want to thank my husband, Mark, for all of his support and love over the years. More than anything else, he has enabled me to maintain my independent lifestyle. He has also supported me all the way along in putting together this memoir. I will love always, Mark Jackson.